*BIBLIOTHECA JAINICA*

# THE SACRED BOOKS OF THE JAINAS

## VOLUME 7

AMS PRESS
NEW YORK

# THE SACRED BOOKS
OF THE
# JAINAS
## Vol. VII
# ATMANUSHASANA
(DISCOURSE TO THE SOUL)

BY

SHRI GUNA-BHADRA ACHARYA

EDITED WITH

TRANSLATION & COMMENTARIES

BY

RAI BAHADUR J. L. JAINI, M. A., BAR-AT-LAW,
*Author of Outlines of Jainism, Jaina Law, Jaina Gem-Dictionary, Gommatsara, Jiva-Kanda & Karma-Kanda, etc., etc.,*

ASSISTED BY

JAIN-DHARMA BHUSHANA BRAHMACHARI SITAL PRASADA JI
EDITOR "JAINA MITRA" AUTHOR OF GRIHASTHA DHARMA, ANUBHAVANANDA, ATMA DHARMA, ETC., ETC.

PUBLISHED BY

**PANDIT AJIT PRASAD, M. A., LL. B.**
THE CENTRAL JAINA PUBLISHING HOUSE
AJITASHRAM, LUCKNOW (INDIA).

**1928.**

Library of Congress Cataloging in Publication Data

Guṇabhadra, 9th cent.
Atmanushasana (Discourse to the soul).
English and Sanskrit.
Original ed. issued as v. 7 of the Sacred books of the Jainas.
1. Jainism. I. Jaini, Jagmandar Lal, d. 1927, ed.
II. Sital Prasad, Brahmachari, ed. III. Title.
IV. Series: The Sacred books of the Jainas, v. 7.
BL1311.A8G8613 1974 294.4′8 73-3841
ISBN 0-404-57707-5

*Original pagination has been maintained.*

Reprinted from the edition of 1928, Lucknow
First AMS edition published, 1974
Manufactured in the United States of America

International Standard Book Number:
Complete Set: 0-404-57700-8
Volume 7: 0-404-57707-5

AMS PRESS, INC.
NEW YORK, N.Y. 10003

## PUBLISHER'S NOTE.

The Great mind which rendered into English, the Great Discourse of Shri Guṉa-Bhadra-Áchárya, left the corporeal tenement known as J. L. Jaini, long before this rendering, which is now presented to the public, was out of the printer's hand.

We are thus deprived of the Author's preface. And those who have read his prefaces, introducing the two volumes of Gommatsára know, what a condensed essence of learning, what a fascinating presentment of matter, subtle and sublime, the introductory passages from the pen of J. L. Jaini, contain.

Atmánushásana is, as the very name literally indicates, a discourse divine for the Divinity in man. Each and every one of the 270 verses, is an exhortation in language, simple, persuasive, penetrating, forceful, and effective, to the Átman, the I, the Ego, the Self, to separate its own Self from the non-Átman, the non-I, the non-Ego, the non-Self. This supreme separation is the complete victory of the Soul over Sin, Sorrow, and Death, and is Moksha, Freedom, or Liberation, absolute, perfect, eternal, and everlasting.

AJITASHRAM, LUCKNOW,
Phálguṉa Púrṉimá, 2453. V. S.
The 6th March, 1928 A. D.

AJIT PRASADA.

# THE SACRED BOOKS OF THE JAINAS.

# आत्मानुशासनम्

## ATMANUSHASANA.

मङ्गलाचरणम्

लक्ष्मीनिवासनिलयं विलीनविलयं निधाय हृदि वीरम् ।
आत्मानुशासनमहं वक्ष्ये मोक्षाय भव्यानाम् ॥ १ ॥

### BENEDICTION.

1. Cherishing in the heart Víra (Mahavíra the 24th Tirthankara), who is the place of residence of Lakshmi (perfection), whose sins have been destroyed, I describe Átmánushásana for the attainment of liberation by those who are capable of being liberated.

**Commentary.**

*Vira.* The last Tírthankara Mahavíra Svámí is often referred to by four other names, Víra, Vardhamána, Ati-víra, and Sanmati. *Lakshmi* is the goddess presiding over riches, knowledge, science, and arts in perfection. The word as used here refers to the attainment of inherent perfection, infinite-conation, infinite-knowledge, infinite-power and infinite-happiness, etc. It also refers to the Super-glory of the Hall of Audience (Samosarana) of the Lord, where the Arhats preside and where discourses emanate from him.

*Atmanushasana*, is the name of this book. Literally, it means Self-culture, or Self-education.

*Bhavyanam.* For the good of the Liberable that is, those who are inclined to listen and derive benefit from the discourses hereby given.

दुःखाद्बिभेषि नितरामभिवाञ्छसि सुखमतोऽहमप्यात्मन् ।
दुःखापहारि सुखकरमनुशास्मि तवानुमतमेव ॥ २ ॥

2. Oh soul ! thou art always afraid of pain, and desirous of pleasure. Therefore I also offer thee the object of thy desire, which tends to give pleasure and remove pain.

यद्यपि कदाचिदस्मिन् विपाकमधुरं तदा तु कटु किञ्चित् ।
त्वं तस्मान्मा भैषीर्यथातुरो भेषजादुग्रात् ॥ ३ ॥

3. If perchance, in this (advice), there be something which though sweet at fruition, is yet unpalatable, be thou not afraid of that, just as a sick person is not (afraid) of bitter medicine.

जना घनाश्च वाचालाः सुलभाः स्युर्वृथोत्थिताः ।
दुर्लभा ह्यन्तरार्द्रास्ते जगदभ्युज्जिहीर्षवः ॥ ४ ॥

4. Persons, who are vain and full of talk, and clouds which thunder but give no rain, are easy to find. But it is difficult to find those kind-hearted persons who desire to uplift the world, just as it is difficult to find clouds, full of rain and beneficial to the world.

प्राज्ञः प्राप्तसमस्तशास्त्रहृदयः प्रव्यक्तलोकस्थितिः
प्रास्ताशः प्रतिभापरः प्रशमवान् प्रागेव दृष्टोत्तरः ।
प्रायः प्रश्नसहः प्रभुः परमनोहारी परानिन्दया
ब्रूयाद्धर्मकथां गणी गुणनिधिः प्रस्पष्टमिष्टाक्षरः ॥ ५ ॥

5. He, who is wise, well-versed in the essence of the Jaina scriptures, aware of the ways of the world, with no sense-desires, brilliant, calm-minded, ever ready with answers, patient of a volley of questions, powerful, attracting other minds, leader of Saints, a repository of good qualities, and with speech clear and sweet, should deliver religious discourses without speaking ill of others.

श्रुतमविकलं शुद्धा वृत्तिः परप्रतिबोधने
परिणतिरुरूद्योगो मार्गप्रवर्त्तनसद्विधौ ।
बुधनुतिरनुत्सेको लोकज्ञता मृदुता स्पृहा
यतिपतिगुणा यस्मिन्नन्ये च सोऽस्तु गुरुः सताम् ॥ ६ ॥

6. Perfect knowledge of the scripture; pure conduct; inclination to pursuade others (to the right path); keen interest in the propagation of the right path (of liberation); obeisance to the learned; pride-less-ness; knowledge of the world; gentleness; desire-less-ness; whoever possesses these and other qualities of the leader of ascetics, be he the Teacher of worthy people.

**Commentary.**

In Shlokas 5 and 6 the highest qualities of a model expounder of the scriptures in the highest degree are given. The relation between the teacher and the taught is, however, a comparative one and it is not meant by the above Shlokas to exclude or disqualify one who does not possess the above qualities in the fullest degree, from expounding the principles of Truth to those whose knowledge is inferior to his.

भव्यः किं कुशलं ममेति विमृशन् दुःखाद्भृशं भीतिमान्
सौख्यैषी श्रवणादिबुद्धिविभवः श्रुत्वा विचार्य्य स्फुटम् ।
धर्म्मं शर्म्मकरं दयागुणमयं युक्त्यागमाभ्यां स्थितम्
गृह्णन् धर्मकथां श्रुतावधिकृतः शास्यो निरस्ताग्रहः ॥ ७ ॥

7. The promising one, who ponders over the summumbonum for the self, is very anxious to avoid (worldly) sufferings, seeks happiness, whose intellectual greatness lies in listening, (retaining) etc., who having heard properly meditates upon Truth, which brings (eternal) happiness, is full of the quality of compassion, and is established by reason, and scriptural authority, and (then) accepts the sacred doctrine, being guided by the scriptures, and rid of obstinacy——such a person is worthy of being taught.

पापाद्दुःखं धर्मात्सुखमिति सर्वजनसुप्रसिद्धमिदम् ।
तस्माद्विहाय पापं चरतु सुखार्थी सदा धर्म्मम् ॥ ८ ॥

8. Demerit produces pain, happiness follows Truth (Dharma). This is well-known to all. Therefore the man who desires happiness should always refrain from demerit, (and) follow Dharma.

सर्वः प्रेप्सति सत्सुखाप्तिमचिरात् सा सर्वकर्मक्षयात्
सद्वृत्तात्स च तच्च बोधनियतं सोऽप्यागमात्स श्रुतेः ।
सा चाप्तात् स च सर्वदोषरहितो रागादयस्तेऽप्यत-
स्तं युक्त्या सुविचार्य्य सर्वसुखदं सन्तः श्रयन्तु श्रियै ॥ ९ ॥

9. All men desire the early attainment of true happiness; it arises from the destruction of all Karmas. (This destruction of the Karmas results) from right conduct; that (right conduct) depends upon (right)

knowledge. And that (right knowledge is acquired) from the Scriptures. The (scriptures are based) on Discourses, (Jinaváni), and this (Jina-váni emanates) from the discoursing Omniscient (Ápta Arhat), and that (Ápta) is free from all defects. These (defects) are attachment and others. Therefore after duly reasoned-out contemplation of Him, the source of all happiness, let the worthy resort to him for their benefit.

**Commentary.**

Jina-Váni is the speech of the Arhat. It is letterless sound, Anakshari Váni, emanating from the Vibratory Omniscient, is understandable by all present, in their own language, being then transformed into lettered discourse.

The defects are eighteen and they are not found in an Omniscient. They are :—

1. Kshudá = Hunger.
2. Trishná = Thirst.
3. Jará = Old age.
4. Átank = Disease.
5. Janma = Birth.
6. Marana = Death.
7. Bhaya = Tear.
8. Smaya = Wonder.
9. Rága = Love.
10. Dvesha = Hate.
11. Moha = Delusion.
12. Rati = Indulgence.
13. Arati = Ennui.
14. Chintá = Anxiety.
15. Sveda = Perspiration.
16. Kheda = Distress.
17. Nidrá = Sleep.
18. Shoka = Sorrow.

श्रद्धानं द्विविधं त्रिधा दशविधं मौढ्याद्यपोढं सदा
संवेगादिविवर्द्धितं भवहरं त्र्यज्ञानशुद्धिप्रदम् ।
निश्चिन्वन् नव सप्त तत्त्वमचलप्रासादमारोहतां
सोपानं प्रथमं विनेय विदुषामाद्येयमाराधना ॥ १० ॥

**10.** Right belief is of two, three, and ten kinds. It is always free from the defects of ignorance, etc., it is overflowing with apprehension of mundane miseries, etc.; (it is the) destroyer of the cycle of existences; purifier of three kinds of wrong knowledge (*i. e.* transforms them into three right kinds of knowledge); it rightly ascertains the seven or the nine principles (tattvas). It is the first step for those who ascend up to the unshakeable fortress (of Liberation). It is, indeed, the first Devotion (Árádhaná) for the learned scholars.

### Commentary.

Right-belief is of two kinds. Intuitive (Nisargaja), or tuitive (Adhigamaja). Nisargaja is self-born, inspired, intutive. Adhigamaja is acquired by study, precept, etc., tuitive. It is of 3 kinds having regard to internal causes, *viz.*, (1) subsidential, aupashamika, in consequence of the subsidence of 4 error-feeding passions and wrong belief, (2) destructive-subsidential (Kshāyopa-Shamika), in consequence of their destructive-subsidence, (3) destructive (Kshayáka) as a consequence of their total destruction. See Tattvártha Sútra, page 5, Chapter I., S.B.J. Vol. II; and Gommaṭasára: Jíva Káṉḍa, Chapter I. pp. 21, 22, S. B. J., Vol. V.

Defects of ignorance, etc.—There are 25 such defects, which should be got rid of, for the purification of right belief. They are the following:—

1. Doubt or fear, 2. Sense-ignorance, 3. Disgust, 4. Superstition, 5. Libel, 6. Non-support to slipping souls, 7. Non-affection for the worthy, 8. Indifference to propagation of Truth ... ... ... ... 8

Pride in 1. Knowledge, 2. Position, 3. Paternal lineage, 4. Maternal family, 5. Strength, 6. Wealth, 7. Asceticism, and 8 Beauty ... ... ... ... ... 8

Blind faith in 1. Popular rites, 2. Unworshipable deties, and 3. Unworthy saints ... ... ... ... 3

Association with 1. Unworshipable deities, 2. Unworthy saints, 3. Misleading scriptures, or with the followers of the above three ... ... ... ... 6

25

For a detailed description of seven, or nine principles, consult Tattvártha Sútra, pp. 6 and 7 in Chapter, I, S.B.J, Vol. II.

**आज्ञामार्गसमुद्भवमुपदेशात्सूत्रबीजसंक्षेपात् ।**
**विस्तारार्थाभ्यां भवमवगाढपरमवगाढे च ॥ ११ ॥**

11. (Right-belief) arises from 1. Ájná, 2. Márga, 3. Updesha, 4. Sútra, 5. Bíja, 6. Sankshepa, 7. Vistára, and 8. Artha; and is either 9. Avagádha and 10, Parmávagádha. (These are the 10 kinds referred to in Shloka 10, above).

आज्ञासम्यक्त्वमुक्तं यदुत विरुचितं वीतरागाज्ञयैव
त्यक्तग्रंथप्रपञ्चं शिवममृतपथं श्रद्दधन्मोहशान्तेः ।
मार्गश्रद्धानमाहुः पुरुषवरपुराणोपदेशोपजाता
या संज्ञानागमाब्धिप्रसृतिभिरुपदेशादिरादेशदृष्टिः ॥ १२ ॥

12. *Ajna* belief is said to be that which is based solely upon the precept of the passionless (saint).

*Marga* belief is said to be the belief in the peaceful, path of eternal liberation, which is free from temporal ties and which arises from the subsidence of the deluding Karmas.

*Updesha or Adesha* belief is that which arises from ancient teachings, of great men, and from sayings, etc., received from the ocean of scriptures of right-knowledge.

आकर्ण्याचारसूत्रं मुनिचरणविधेः सूचनं श्रद्दधानः
सूक्तासौ सूत्रदृष्टिर्दुरधिगमगतेरर्थसार्थस्य बीजैः ।
कैश्चिज्जातोपलब्धेरसमशमवशाद्बीजदृष्टिः पदार्थात्
संक्षेपेणैव बुध्वा रुचिमुपगतवान्साधुसंक्षेपदृष्टिः ॥ १३ ॥

13. *Sutra* belief is well said to be possessed by one who believes in rules declared for the conduct of ascetics, on hearing books on discipline.

*Bija* belief is that which arises from the knowledge of substances, difficult to understand, (but) known with the help of certain symbols, as a result of the subsidence of perverse belief.

*Sankshepa* belief is the laudable belief possessed by one who has acquired faith (in principles) only explained summarily.

यः श्रुत्वा द्वादशाङ्गीं कृतरुचिरथ तं विद्धि विस्तारदृष्टिं
संजातार्थात् कुतश्चित् प्रवचनवचनान्यन्तरेणार्थदृष्टिः ।

दृष्टिः साङ्गाङ्गबाह्यप्रवचनभवगाह्योत्थिता यावगाढा
कैवल्यालोकितार्थे रुचिरिह परमावगाढेति रूढा ॥ १४ ॥

14. *Vistara* belief should be known to be possessed by one who has acquired faith, after having heard the twelve Angas (Jaina Sacred lore).

*Artha* belief is that which is produced by (ascertaining the true, real meaning of the sacred books, independently of words.

*Avagadha* belief is that which is produced by a thorough study of the sacred literature of the Angas and of that outside the Angas.

*Pramavagadha* is popularly known to be the belief in substances as seen by Omniscients.

शमबोधवृत्ततपसां पाषाणस्येव गौरवं पुंसः ।
पूज्यं महामणेरिव तदेव सम्यक्त्वसंयुक्तम् ॥ १५ ॥

15. The tranquillity, knowledge, vows, and austerities of a person is of the value of a stone. But it becomes adorable, like a great jewel if accompanied by right belief.

**Commentary.**

Knowledge, vows, austerities are forms of knowledge and conduct. But to be right, they must be preceded by right-belief. Then alone they become right knowledge and right conduct, which with right-belief are the three Jewels of Jainism.

मिथ्यात्वातङ्कवतो हिताहितप्राप्त्यनाप्तिमुग्धस्य ।
बालस्येव तवेयं सुकुमारैव क्रिया क्रियते ॥ १६ ॥

16. Only this gentle remedy is prescribed, as for a child, for thee, who art a sufferer from the disease of wrong-belief, and does not know what good is to be pursued, and what evil is to be avoided.

विषयविषप्राशनोत्थितमोहज्वरजनिततीव्रतृष्णस्य ।
निःशक्तिकस्य भवतः प्रायः पेयाद्युपक्रमः श्रेयान् ॥ १७ ॥

17. Having taken the poison of sense-enjoyments, thou hast got the fever of delusion; from this has arisen

thy keen thirst (for sense-gratification) and thou hast become feeble. For thee it is the best to be treated mostly with medicines of a drinkable nature.

सुखितस्य दुःखितस्य च संसारे धर्म एव तव कार्य्यः ।
सुखितस्य तदभिवृद्ध्यै दुःखभुजस्तदुपघाताय ॥ १८ ॥

18. Whether happy or miserable in this world, thou must exercise piety; if happy to increase thy happiness; and if miserable, to remove thy misery.

धर्मारामतरूणां फलानि सर्वेन्द्रियार्थसौख्यानि ।
संरक्षतांस्ततस्तान्युच्चिनुयैस्तैरुपायैस्त्वम् ॥ १९ ॥

19. The pleasures derived from all senses-objects are fruits of the trees of the garden of piety. Therefore preserve thou the trees, and pluck the fruits by all means.

धर्मः सुखस्य हेतुर्हेतुर्न विरोधकः स्वकार्य्यस्य ।
तस्मात् सुखभङ्गभिया माभूर्धर्मस्य विमुखस्त्वम् ॥ २० ॥

20. Piety is the cause of happiness. The cause cannot oppose its own effect. Therefore for fear of being deprived of (present) sense-pleasures, thou shouldst not be indifferent to piety (Dharma).

धर्मादवाप्तविभवो धर्मं प्रतिपाल्य भोगमनुभवतु ।
बीजादवाप्तधान्यः कृषीवलास्तस्य बीजमिव ॥ २१ ॥

21. The person who in consequence of piety has acquired prosperity may have enjoyments while preserving piety, like the peasant who gets corn from the seed, but (preserves) the seed of that corn.

संकल्प्यं कल्पवृक्षस्य चिन्त्यं चिन्तामणेरपि ।
असंकल्प्यमसंचिन्त्यं फलं धर्मादवाप्यते ॥ २२ ॥

22. The fruit of the wishing-tree (Kalpa-Vraksha) is got by wishing, that of Chintamani (miraculous gem by thinking; (but) the fruit of piety is obtained without wishing and without thinking.

परिणाममेव कारणमाहुः खलु पुण्यपापयोः प्राज्ञाः ।
तस्मात् पापापचयः पुण्योपचयश्च सुविधेयः ॥ २३ ॥

23. The wise men say that thought-activity only is the cause of merit and demerit. Therefore one should carefully destroy demerits and accumulate merits.

कृत्वा धर्मविघातं विषयसुखान्यनुभवन्ति ये मोहात् ।
आच्छिद्य तरुं मूलात्फलानि गृह्णन्ति ते पापाः ॥ २४ ॥

24. Those who under delusion, destroying Dharma, enjoy sense-pleasures are sinful, and take the fruit (after) cutting down the tree at its root.

कर्तृत्वहेतुकर्तृत्वानुमतैः स्मरणचरणवचनेषु ।
यः सर्वथाभिगम्यः स कथं धर्मो न संग्राह्यः ॥ २५ ॥

25. Why should such a religion be not pursued, which can be followed in all circumstances, by doing, by having it done, and by approving the doing of it by others, by means of mind, body, or speech?

धर्मो वसेन्मनसि यावदलं स ताव-
द्धन्ता न हन्तुरपि पश्य गतेऽथ तस्मिन् ।
दृष्टा परस्परहतिर्जनकात्मजानां
रक्षा ततोऽस्य जगतः खलु धर्म एव ॥ २६ ॥

26. So long as piety abides well in the heart, the man does not slay even his slayer. When that religion goes away, the father and the son are found killing each other. Therefore the protection of this world depends verily upon Dharma only.

न सुखानुभवात्पापं पापं तद्धेतुघातकारम्भात् ।
नाजीर्णं मिष्टान्नान्ननु तन्मात्राद्यतिक्रमणात् ॥ २७ ॥

27. There is no demerit in enjoying pleasures; but there is demerit in doing what tends to destroy their source. Indigestion is not caused by sweet food, (but) by eating it beyond its limit.

अप्येतन्मृगयादिकं यदि तव प्रत्यक्षदुःखास्पदम्
पापैराचरितं पुरातिभयदं सौख्याय संकल्पतः ।
संकल्पं तमनुज्झितेन्द्रियसुखैरासेविते धीधनै—
र्धर्मे (र्म्ये)कर्मणि किं करोति न भवान् लोकद्वयश्रेयसि ॥ २८ ॥

28. When thou takest a pleasure in all this hunting, etc., which produce much fear in the very beginning, which evidently cause pain, and which are pursued by sinners, why dost thou not take the same view of piety, which is for the good of both the (present and future) worlds, which is pursued by those who are rich in wisdom, and have not abandoned sense-enjoyments.

भीतमूर्तीगतत्राणा निर्दोषा देहवित्तिका ।
दन्तलग्नतृणा घ्नन्ति मृगीरन्येषु का कथा ॥ २६ ॥

29. An image of fear, unprotected, innocent, with her body as her sole property, with grass blades between her teeth—even such a she-deer is killed (by hunters); what to say of others !

पैशून्यदैन्यदम्भस्तेयानृतपातकादिपरिहारात् ।
लोकद्वयहितमर्जय धर्मार्थयशःसुखायार्थम् ॥ ३० ॥

30. Having given up back-biting, begging, deceit, theft, falsehood and other faults, pursue what is best in both the worlds for religion, wealth, renown and happiness.

पुण्यं कुरुष्व कृतपुण्यमनीदृशोऽपि
नोपद्रवोऽभिभवति प्रभवेच्च भूत्यै ।
संतापयन् जगदशेषमशीतरश्मिः
पद्मेषु पश्य विदधाति विकाशलक्ष्मीम् ॥ ३१ ॥

31. Acquire merit. Even an unheard of calamity does not affect the doer of meritorious deeds. Indeed it does him good. See the sun, which oppresses the whole world (with its heat), gives a lovely bloom to lotuses.

नेता यस्य (यत्र) बृहस्पतिः प्रहरणं वज्रं सुराः सैनिकाः
स्वर्गो दुर्गमनुग्रहः खलु हरेरैरावतो वारणः ।
इत्याश्चर्यबलान्वितोऽपि बलभिद्भग्नः परैः संगरे
तद्व्यक्तं ननु दैवमेव शरणं धिग्धिग्वृथा पौरुषम् ॥ ३२ ॥

32. Whose guide was Brihaspati, whose weapon was the thunder-bolt, whose soldiers were celestial beings, whose fortress was heaven, who was certainly in the favour of Hari (Krishna) and whose elephant was Airavata —even with such wonderful forces, Indra was defeated in battle by others. From this, it is certainly evident that destiny is the only protection and futile endeavour (to change this destiny) is contemptible.

**Commentary.**

The above illustration is from-non-Jaina literature, and is given for the purpose of showing that under the strong operation of Karmas, even Indra in spite of his vast resources and prowess was defeated in battle. Stress has been laid on the inevitable effect of Karmas, with a view to impress upon those who are infatuated with their wordly possessions and power, and are oblivious of the approaching and inevitable Death, the urgent need of adopting the course of right conduct. It does not mean that personal endeavour is always futile. The effect of Karmas can certainly be altered by pious deeds and thoughts. One should not, therefore, make any delay in adopting the rules of discipline laid down in the Scriptures, lest Death should suddenly overcome, and deprive him of the valuable and rare opportunity of self advancement.

भर्त्तारः कुलपर्वता इव भुवो मोहं विहाय स्वयं
रत्नानां निधयः पयोधय इव व्यावृत्तवित्तस्पृहाः ।
स्पृष्टाः कैरपि नो नभोविभुतयाविश्वस्य विश्रान्तये
सन्त्यद्यापि चिरन्तनान्तिकचराः सन्तः कियन्तोऽप्यमी ॥३३॥

33. Some worthy disciples of the ancient sages exist even to-day. These, having themselves destroyed all delusion, have become protectors of (people), like Kuláchalas (the mounts Himavana, Mahahimana, etc., protecting the terristrial regions, Bharata, Haimavata

etc). They are the respositories of the jewels (of attributes) like the oceans, having vanquished all desire for wealth. They are not touched by (attachment for) anything whatsoever. Majestic, like space, they are a source of peace to all.

**Commentary.**

Reference is made to living ascetics and sages in order to persuade the listener to get rid of delusion, and temporal attachment, and to adopt a pious course of life.

पिता पुत्रं पुत्रः पितरमभिसंधाय बहुधा
विमोहादीहेते सुखलवमवाप्तुं नृपपदम् ।
अहो मुग्धो लोको मृतिजननदंष्ट्रान्तरगतो
न पश्यत्यश्रान्तं तनुमपहरन्तं यममसुम् ॥ ३४ ॥

34. Being moved with the desire of getting Kingship, (which is only a small) bit of pleasure, the father often tries to cheat his son, and the son the father. It is strange that this foolish world, which is fallen between the jaws of birth and death, does not see yonder Death indefatigably snatching away the body.

अन्धादयं महानन्धो विषयान्धीकृतेक्षणः ।
चक्षुषान्धो न जानाति विषयान्धो न केनचित् ॥ ३५ ॥

35. One whose eyes are blinded by sense-desire is the blindest of the blind. The blind man cannot see with the eye (only), while one, blinded by sense-desires cannot (perceive) through any means.

आशागर्त्तः प्रतिप्राणि यस्मिन् विश्वमणूपमम् ।
कस्य किं कियदायाति वृथा वो विषयैषिता ॥ ३६ ॥

36. Every living being (has such a deep) pit of worldly desires that (all objects in) the world (amount to) only a particle for it. What, and how much, then, can each get ? Useless (is) your desire of sense-enjoyments.

आयुश्रीवपुरादिकं यदि भवेत्पुण्यं पुरोपार्जितम्
स्यात्सर्वं न भवेन्न तच्च नितरामायासितेऽप्यात्मनि ।

इत्यार्य्याः सुविचार्य्य कार्य्यकुशलाः कार्य्येऽत्र मन्दोद्यमाः
द्रागागामीभवार्थमेव सततं प्रीत्या यतन्तेतराम् ॥ ३७ ॥

37. (Long) life, wealth, (strong and well-built) body etc., are all possible if merit has been acquired in the past; if not, they are not possible even if the soul under goes unremitting labour (to attain them). Thus gentlemen, proficient in practical matters, after proper consideration, exert themselves mildly for wordly matters; but cheerfully take prompt and continuous measures for the life hereafter.

कः स्वादो विषयेष्वसौ कटुविषप्रख्येष्वलं दुःखिना
यानन्वेष्टुमिव त्वयाशुचिकृतं येनाभिमानामृतम् ।
आज्ञातं करणैर्मनःप्रणिधिभिः पित्तज्वराविष्टवत्
कष्टं रागरसैः सुधीस्त्वमपि सन् व्यत्यासितास्वादनः ॥ ३८ ॥

38. What pleasure is there in sense-gratifications, which are well-known as bitter like poison, that thou, being distressed in the search for them hast grossly defiled the nectar of thy self-respect? Enthralled by the senses, attendant upon the mind, (and) like one possessed by bilious fever, thou, alas! though wise, hast got perverted taste by the enjoyment of (worldly) attachments.

अनिवृत्तेर्जगत्सर्वं मुखादवशिनष्टि यत् ।
तत्तस्याशक्तितो भोक्तुं वितनोर्भानुसोमवत् ॥ ३९ ॥

39. (The fact) that the whole world has been saved from the mouth of one, who has renounced nothing, is because of his non-capacity for taking in (the whole of) it, just as the sun and the moon (have been saved from the mouth) of Rahu, a planet.

### Commentary.

The point in the above shloka is that the sense-desires are so strong and various that one would wish to appropriate all objects of worldly enjoyments, but as his capacity for enjoyment is limited, he can enjoy only a very small part of them. The allusion is to the Indian astronomical belief that Rahu, a planet, occasionally attempts to eat up the sun, and the moon, but fails in doing so because of his own incapacity in gulping them down. The moral is that sense-desires, infructuous as they are, should be duly restrained, and all energy should be directed towards self-control and acts of piety, beneficial here, and hereafter.

साम्राज्यं कथमप्यवाप्य सुचिरात्संसारसारं पुन-
स्तत्त्यक्त्वैव यदि क्षितीश्वरवराः प्राप्ताः श्रियं शाश्वतीम् ।
त्वं प्रागेव परिग्रहान्परिहर त्याज्यान् गृहीत्वापि ते
माभूर्भौतिकमोदकव्यतिकरं संपाद्य हास्यास्पदम् ॥ ४० ॥

**40.** Having after a long time and some how obtained the position of an Emperor (Chakravarti), the best (of all positions) in the world, the mighty monarchs obtained eternal bliss only by its renunciation. Thou shouldst (then) from the beginning renounce wordly entanglements, which are fit to be discarded. Be not thou an object of ridicule like (the person in the garb of) an ascetic (who rendered himself an object of) ridicule (by taking up) a sweet ball (which had fallen in filth, and who said that he would not eat it but would throw it away after washing it).

**Commentary.**

The moral inculcated in this Shloka is that one should under no pretence or temptation take to worldly objects, which must be renounced as early as possible to enable one to attain liberation.

सर्वं धर्ममयं क्वचित् क्वचिदपि प्रायेण पापात्मकम्
क्वाप्येतद्द्वयवत्करोति चरितं प्रज्ञाधनानामपि ।
तस्मादेष तदन्धरज्जुवलनं स्नानं गजस्याथवा
मत्तोन्मत्तविचेष्टितं न हि हितो गेहाश्रमः सर्वथा ॥ ४१ ॥

**41.** The household stage makes the stage life of even those who are rich in wisdom, sometimes of meritorious, sometimes all sinful, and sometimes both; it is thus like the making of a rope by the blind, or the bathing of an elephant, or the act of a mad man. It is not wholly beneficial.

**Commentary.**

The numerous cares and engagements of household affairs do not allow one a suitable opportunity for spiritual advancement. A blind person, while twisting a rope by one end, goes on untwisting it at the other ; an elephant covers himself with dust soon after he is washed ; and a madman's efforts are directed to no useful purpose. Similarly a person engaged in household affairs can not adopt the calm and contemplative conduct necessary for the attainment of eternal bliss.

कृष्ट्वोप्त्वा नृपतीन्निषेव्य बहुशो भ्रान्त्वा वनेऽम्भोनिधौ
किं क्लिश्नासि सुखार्थमत्र सुचिरं हा कष्टमज्ञानतः ।
तैलं त्वं सिकतासु यन्मृगयसे वाञ्छेद् विषाज्जीवितुं
नन्वाशाग्रहनिग्रहात्तव सुखं न ज्ञातमेतत्त्वया ॥ ४२ ॥

**42.** It is a great pity that thou shouldst out of ignorance make thyself miserable so long in the world by ploughing and sowing the land, by serving kings in many ways, and by wandering about in jungles and on the seas, in pursuit of pleasure. Thou wishest (to get) oil from sand; thou wishest to live on poison. Dost thou not know that thy happiness lies in subduing the demon of desires ?

आशाहुताशनग्रस्तवस्त्वर्थी (स्तूच्चैः) वंशजां जनाः ।
हा किलैति (त्य) सुखच्छायां दुःखघर्मापनोद (दि) नः ॥ ४३ ॥

**43.** It is a pity that a person actuated by burning desires, should for comfort take to objects of sense-gratification, which would give him no comfort, but (like one who) being oppressed by the sun, seeks the shade of bamboo-trees, (which give no shade, but get ignited by friction).

खातेऽभ्यासजलाशयाजनि शिला प्रारब्धनिर्वाहिणा
भूयोभेदि रसातलावधि ततः कृच्छ्रात्सुतुच्छं किल ।
क्षारं वार्युदगात्तदप्युपहतं पूतिकृमिश्रेणिभिः
शुष्कं तच्च पिपासितोऽस्य सहसा कष्टं विधेश्चेष्टितम् ॥ ४४ ॥

**44.** With a will to complete what he had begun, a man with a desire to get water began digging and by dint of labour struck a rock. Yet he went on digging down the nether world. Then he got only a little brackish water with great difficulty. That also was stinking and full of worms, and dried up quickly. So awful was the effect of this thirsty man's ill luck.

शुद्धैर्धनैर्विवृद्धन्ते सतामपि न संपदः ।
न हि स्वच्छाम्बुभिः पूर्णाः कदाचिदपि सिंधवः ॥ ४५ ॥

45. The wealth of even good men is not increased by pious income; (as) the seas can never be filled with fresh water only.

**Commentary.**

It is impossible to earn money while observing a conduct, which may not cause any injury or pain to any living being. The different occupations of agriculture, trade and industry, etc., inevitably involve the causing of pain to innumerable living beings, by which demeritorious Karmas are bound. One must therefore give up all household occupations in order to purify his soul.

स धर्मो यत्र नाधर्मस्तत्सुखं यत्र नासुखम् ।
तज्ज्ञानं यत्र नाज्ञानं सा गतिर्यत्र नागतिः ॥ ४६ ॥

46. Dharma is that where there is no Adharma. Happiness is that, where there is no un-happiness, knowledge is that, where there is no ignorance. Condition of existence is that, whence there is no coming back (to the world).

वार्त्तादिभिर्विषयलोलविचारशून्यः
क्लिश्नासि यन्मुहुरिहार्थपरिग्रहार्थम् ।
तच्चेष्टितं यदि सकृत्परलोकबुद्ध्या
न प्राप्यते ननु पुनर्जननादि दुःखम् ॥ ४७ ॥

47. Being entangled in enjoyments, (and therefore) thoughtless, thou art again and again made miserable by occupation, etc., to obtain wealth and other objects of this world. If thou under-goest the same trouble (even) once, intending to obtain liberation, then certainly thou wouldst never experience the pain of being born again and again.

संकल्प्येदमनिष्टमिष्टमिदमित्यज्ञातयाथात्मको
बाह्ये वस्तुनि किं वृथैव गमयस्यासज्य कालं मुहुः ।
अन्तः शान्तिमुपैहि यावदुदयप्राप्तान्तकप्रस्फुर-
ज्ज्वालाभीषणजाठरानलमुखे भस्मीभवेन्नो भवान् ॥ ४८ ॥

48. Ignorant of the true nature of things, considering some to be desirable and others undesirable, why dost thou waste thy time being often attached to external things again and again. Attain to internal peace of mind before you are reduced to ashes in the cruel and approaching Death's abdominal fire, horrible with its leaping flames.

आयातोऽस्यति दूरतोऽङ्ग ! परवानाशासरित्प्रेरितः
किन्नावैषि ननु त्वमेव नितरामेनां तरीतुं क्षमः ।
स्वातन्त्र्यं व्रज यासि तीरमचिरान्नोचेद्दुरन्तान्तक-
ग्राहव्यात्तगभीरवक्त्रविषमे मध्ये भवाब्धेर्भवेः ॥ ४९ ॥

49. Oh friend! dependent upon external things (and) floating in the river of desire, thou hast come down from a long long distance. Dost thou not know that thou thyself art quite capable of crossing this river easily? Be independent, (and) thou shalt reach the shore very soon; otherwise, thou shalt founder in the ocean of existence, which is terrible on account of the deep and wide-open mouth of the unvanquishable crocodile of death.

आस्वाद्याद्य यदुज्झितं विषयिभिर्व्यावृत्तकौतूहलै-
स्तद्भूयोऽप्यविकुत्सयन्नभिलषस्यप्राप्तपूर्वं यथा ।
जन्तो किं तव शान्तिरस्ति न भवान्यावद्दुराशामिमा-
मंहःसंहतिवीरवैरिपृतनाश्रीवैजयन्तीं हरेत् ॥ ५० ॥

50. Thou desirest now, without any revulsion (to pick up) again, as if thou hadst never tasted before, what has been discarded by the sensualists, after the satiety of enjoyment. Oh soul! canst thou gain peace so long as thou

dost not conquer this desire-evil which is the victory banner of the forces of (your) powerful enemy, the host of sins.

भंक्त्वा भाविभवांश्च भोगिविषमान् भोगान् बुभुक्षुर्भृशं
मृत्वापि स्वयमस्तभीतिकरुणः सर्वाञ्जिघांसुर्मुधा ।
यद्यत्साधुविगर्हितं हतमिति तस्यैव धिक्कामुकः
कामक्रोधमहाग्रहाहितमनाः किं किं न कुर्याज्जनः ॥ ५१ ॥

51. Fie on the wretch who having lost fear (of the next world) and compassion, keenly desires sense-enjoyments, which are terrible like serpents, and having ruined his future lives, foolishly kills all (happiness by himself, dying an (impious death), and who desires all that which is censured by the saints! what may not a person do, whose mind has been influenced by the great demon of desire and anger.

श्वो यस्याजनि यः स एव दिवसो ह्यस्तस्य संपद्यते
स्थैर्यं नाम न कस्यचिज्जगदिदं कालानिलोन्मूलितम् ।
भ्रातर्भ्रान्तिमपास्य पश्यसितरां प्रत्यक्षमक्ष्णोर्न किं
येनात्रैव मुहुर्मुहुर्बहुतरं बद्धस्पृहो भ्राम्यसि ॥ ५२ ॥

52. That same day which appears as to-morrow for one, becomes yesterday for him. Nothing can be called stable. This world is being uprooted by the wind of time. Oh brother, having given up delusion, why dost thou not see what is visible to thy eyes. By not doing so, thou, mainly a bondsman of desire, wanderest again and again, in this very world.

संसारे नरकादिषु स्मृतिपथेऽप्युद्वेगकारीण्यलं
दुःखानि प्रतिसेवितानि भवता तान्येवमेवासताम् ।
तत्तावत्स्मरसि (स) स्मरस्मितशितापाङ्गैरनङ्गायुधै-
र्वामानां हिमदग्धमुग्धतरुवद्यत्प्राप्तवान्निर्धनः ॥ ५३ ॥

53. In this world you have suffered many miseries in hell and elsewhere, so much that even their recollection

is excruciating. Let them be just as they are. Dost thou then remember that, like a young sapling blasted by frost, thou art made a pauper by the piercing glances and lovely smiles of females, (which are the) weapons of Cupid.

उत्पन्नोऽस्यति दोषधातुमलवद्देहोऽसि कोपादिवान्
साधिव्याधिरसि प्रहीणचरितोऽस्यस्यात्मनो वञ्चकः ।
मृत्युव्यात्तमुखान्तरोऽसि जरसा ग्रस्तोऽसि जन्मिन् वृथा
किं मत्तोऽस्यसि किं हितारिरहिते किं वासि बद्धस्पृहः ॥ ५४ ॥

**54**. O! living being thou hast taken birth; thou hast assumed a body full of defects and blood and bones, etc.; thou art subject to anger, etc., thou art subject to physical and mental suffering; thy character is very bad, thou art a cheat to thy soul; thou art lying in the wide-open mouth of death; thou art in the clutches of age. Oh why art thou deluded? Why art thou an enemy to thy own good? And why hast thou fixed thy desires on unwholesome things?

उग्रग्रीष्मकठोरघर्मकिरणस्फूर्ज्जद्गभस्तिप्रभैः
संतप्तः सकलेन्द्रियैरयमहो संवृद्धतृष्णो जनः
अप्राप्याभिमतं विवेकविमुखः पापप्रयासाकुल-
स्तोयोपान्तदुरन्तकर्दमगतक्षीणोऽक्षवत् क्लिश्यते ॥ ५५ ॥

**55.** Distressed by all sense-desires, which are gleaming (and blinding) like the sun with its very hot unbearable and scorching rays; keenly athirst with desire; (and) indiscriminate,—this man, not getting his desired object (and) being troubled by sinful exertions, becomes miserable like the weak ox in a deep mire near the edge of a piece of water.

लब्धेन्धनो ज्वलत्यग्निः प्रशाम्यति निरन्धिनः ।
ज्वलत्युभयथाप्युच्चैरहो मोहाग्निरुत्कटः ॥ ५६ ॥

**56.** Fire burns when fed with fuel, and goes out for want of it. But it is a wonder that the terrible fire of delusion blazes strongly in both the ways (on getting the objects of desire and also on not getting them).

किं मर्माण्यभिदन्नभीकरतरो दुष्कर्म्मगर्म्मुद्गणः
किं दुःखज्वलनावली विलसितैर्नालेढि देहश्चिरम् ।
किं गर्ज्जद्यमतूर्य्य (र) भैरवरवान्नाकर्णयन्निर्णयन्
येनायं न जहाति मोहविहितां निद्रामभद्रां जनः ॥ ५७ ॥

57. Has not the exceedingly frightful mace of sinful actions torn the vital parts? Has the body not been licked since long, by the flames of the fires of pain? Has he not veritably heard the terrible sound of the bugles of death. Why then does this man not give up the harmful sleep, caused by delusion.

तादात्म्यं तनुभिः सदानुभवनं पाकस्य दुष्कर्मणो
व्यापारः समयं प्रति प्रकृतिभिर्गाढं स्वयं बन्धनम्
निद्राविश्रमणं मृतेः प्रतिभयं शश्वन्मृतिश्च ध्रुवं
जन्मिन् जन्मनि ते तथापि रमसे तत्रैव चित्रं महत् ॥ ५८ ॥

58. Thou art identified with the bodies; always dost thou experience the fruition of pain-bearing Karmas; thy business is to be closely bound, of thy own accord, at every moment, by the Karma Prakritis, *i. e.*, Karmic matter. Thou feelest rest in sleep; art ever fearful of death, and death is always certain. Oh living being, dost thou still take pleasure in birth. It is this which is very strange.

अस्थिस्थूलतुलाकलापघटितं नद्धं शिरास्नायुभि-
श्चर्माच्छादितमस्रसान्द्रपिशितैर्लिप्तं सुगुप्तं खलैः ।
कर्मारातिभिरायुरुच्चनिगलालग्नं शरीरालयं
कारागारमवेहि ते हतमते प्रीतिं वृथा मा कृथाः ॥ ५९ ॥

59. Know this body of thine to be a prison house, built of a number of thick bones as stone pillars, fastened by nerves and muscles, covered over with skin, plastered

with wet flesh, well-protected by its wicked enemies, the Karmas, and closed by strong barriers of age-Karmas. O Bereft of wisdom ! Have no foolish love for it.

शरणमशरणं वो बन्धवो बन्धमूलं
चिरपरिचितदारा द्वारमापद्गृहाणाम् ।
विपरिमृशत पुत्राः शत्रवः सर्वमेतत्
त्यजत भजत धर्म्मं निर्मलं शर्म्मकामाः ॥ ६० ॥

60. Your house is no protection ; the relations are the cause of bondage ; the wife to whom you have been long attached is the door to abodes of miseries. Know your sons to be your enemies. Forsake all these. Desirous of happiness, you should practise pure religion.

तत्कृत्यं किमिहेन्धनैरिव धनैराशाग्निसंधुक्षणैः
सम्बन्धेन किमङ्ग शश्वदशुभैः सम्बन्धिभिर्बन्धुभिः ।
किं मोहाहिमहाबिलेन सदृशा देहेन गेहेन वा
देहिन् याहि सुखाय ते सममसुं मा गाः प्रमादं मुधा ॥ ६१ ॥

61. What should, in this world, be done with wealth, which, like fuel, feeds the fire of desire ? Oh friend ! What is the use of connection with family and relations who are ever (helpful in acquiring) inauspicious (Karmas) ! What is the use of the body and the home, which are like big holes of the cobra of delusion ! O thou embodied one, for happiness acquire this equanimity, (which is the essence of religion); do not be negligent in vain.

आदावेव महाबलैरविचलं पट्टेन बद्धा स्वयं
रक्षाध्यक्षभुजासिपञ्जरवृता सामन्तसंरक्षिता ।
लक्ष्मीर्दीपशिखोपमा क्षितिमतां हा पश्यतां नश्यति
प्रायः पातितचामरानिलहते वान्यत्र काशा नृणाम् ॥ ६२ ॥

62. Alas, the fortune of rulers of the earth, though it is inextricably bound, in the very beginning, by mighty ones themselves, with (royal) turban, is protected by their vassals, is surrounded, as if it were in a cage, by swords in

the hands of guarding soldiers, perishes, while they remain looking at it, (in the twinkling of an eye), like the flame of a lamp blown off by wind raised by royal fan. In case of what persons can there be hope (of a steady fortune).

दीप्तोभयाग्रवातारिदारूदरगकीटवत् ।
जन्ममृत्युसमाश्लिष्टे शरीरे वत सीदसि ॥ ६३ ॥

63. Alas, thou art tortured in the body, wrapped by birth and death, like an insect inside a castor log burning at both ends.

नेत्रादीश्वरचोदितः सकलुषो रूपादिविश्वाय किं
प्रेष्यः सीदति (सि) कुत्सितव्यतिकरैरंहांस्यलं बृंहयन् ।
नीत्वा तानि भुजिष्यतामकलुषो विश्वं विसृज्यात्मवा-
नात्मानं धिनु सत्सुखी धुतरजाः सद्वृत्तिभिर्निर्वृतः ॥ ६४ ॥

64. Servant of, and instigated by the eye and other rulers (*i. e.*, the senses), and greatly multiplying thy sins by censurable acts, why dost thou miserably distress thyself for beauty and other worldly objects. Having brought them under thy yoke, having renounced the world without regret, having mastered thyself, having washed away the dust (of Karmas) by rule of right conduct, having freed thyself (from mundane existence), and having become supremely happy, enjoy (this bliss of) self-realization.

अर्थिनो धनमप्राप्य धनिनोऽप्यवितृप्तितः ।
कष्टं सर्वेऽपि सीदन्ति परमेको मुनिः सुखी ॥ ६५ ॥

65. The poor are discontented for not obtaining wealth, and the rich too are (so) for want of contentment. Alas! all are in trouble. Only an ascetic is happy.

परायत्तात्सुखाद्दुःखं स्वायत्तं केवलं वरम् ।
अन्यथा सुखिनामानः कथमासंस्तपस्विनः ॥ ६६ ॥

66. Happiness, dependent upon others (leads) to pain. Only independent happiness is commendable. Else how could the ascetics be called happy?

यदेतत्स्वच्छन्दं विहरणमकार्पण्यमशनं
सहार्यैः संवासः श्रुतमुपशमैकश्रमफलम्।
मनो मन्दस्यन्दं बहिरपि चिरायाति विमृशन्
न जाने कस्येयं परिणतिरुदारस्य तपसः ॥ ६७ ॥

67. I do not know of what noble austerities is this the result, that (an ascetic) moves about at will, (gets) food without humility, (has) company of the saints, (has) knowledge with calmness as fruit of hard study, and (his) tranquil mind (being deeply absorbed in) contemplating (upon the self) comes out after long intervals to external (objects).

विरतिरतुला शास्त्रे चिन्ता तथा करुणापरा
मतिरपि सदैकान्तध्वान्तप्रपञ्चविभेदिनी।
अनशनतपश्चर्या चान्ते यथोक्तविधानतो
भवति महतां नाल्पस्येदं फलं तपसो विधेः ॥ ६८ ॥

68. The high-minded (saints) have unique renunciation (of worldly attachments), contemplation of the scriptures, unlimited compassion (towards the living world), also an intellect capable of ever dispelling the illusion of sticking to one-sided view of a thing, and lastly the austerity of fasting according to rules laid down (in the sacred books). This is the result of practising high and not small austerities.

उपायकोटिदूरक्षे स्वतस्तत इतोऽन्यतः।
सर्वतः पतनप्राये काये कोऽयं तवाग्रहः ॥ ६९ ॥

69. What is this attachment of thine for the body, which is altogether destructible, (and) which cannot be saved by millions of remedies (either) from thee (or) from others?

अवश्यं नश्वरैरेभिरायुःकायादिभिर्यदि।
शाश्वतं पदमायाति मुधा यातमवेहि ते ॥ ७० ॥

70. If eternal place (liberation) can be had through these necessarily perishable age, body, etc., then know that thou hast obtained it easily.

गन्तुमुच्छ्वासनिश्वासैरभ्यस्यत्येष सन्ततम् ।
लोकः पृथगितो वाञ्छत्यात्मानमजरामरम् ॥ ७१ ॥

71. This (life) constantly practises to go out by breaths coming in and going out. The people, on the other hand, wish the present life to be undecayable and immortal.

गलत्यायुः प्रायः प्रकटितघटीयन्त्रसलिलं
खलः कायोऽप्यायुर्गतिमनुपतत्येष सततम् ।
किमस्यान्यैरन्यैर्द्वयमयमिदं जीवितमिह-
स्थितो भ्रान्त्या नावि स्वमिव मनुते स्थास्नुमपधीः ॥ ७२ ॥

72. Age, is constantly running out, like water from the bucket of the well-known water-drawing wheel. This wicked body too is always following the course of age. What to say of this soul's friendship with others in this world, (when) these two (body and age) are such (*i. e.*, transient). It is only a fool, who like one sitting in a boat, thinks himself, out of illusion, to be steady.

उच्छ्वासखेदजन्यत्वाद्दुःखमेवात्र जीवितम् ।
तद्विरामे भवेन्मृत्युर्नृणां भण कुतः सुखम् ॥ ७३ ॥

73. Life here is painful on account of the fatigue arising from breathing; on its cessation, there is death. Say where is happiness (then) for human kind.

जन्मतालद्रुमाज्जन्तु फलानि प्रच्युतान्यधः ।
अप्राप्य मृत्युभूभागमन्तरे स्युः कियच्चिरम् ॥ ७४ ॥

74. Living beings are (like) fruits, falling down from the palm-tree of birth. How long can (they) be in the intervening space before they reach the ground of death?

क्षितिजलधिभिः संख्यातीतैर्बहिः पवनैस्त्रिभिः
परिवृतमतः खे नाधस्तात्खलासुरनारकान् ।

उपरि दिविजान्मध्ये कृत्वा नरान्विधिमन्त्रिणा
पतिरपि नृणां त्राता नैको ह्यलंघ्यतमोऽन्तकः ॥ ७५ ॥

75. The minister-Karma has placed evil-minded Asura (kind of celestials) and hellish beings below, the heavenly beings above; and human beings in the middle (of universe) and surrounded them with innumerable continents and oceans, and further with the three sheaths of atmosphere, there is not even one protecting guardian of man-kind. Surely death is the most insurmountable.

अविज्ञातस्थानो व्यपगततनुः पापमलिनः
खलो राहुर्भास्वद्दशशतकराक्रान्तभुवनम् ।
स्फुरन्तं भास्वन्तं किल गिलति हा कष्टमपरं
परिप्राप्ते काले विलसितविधेः को हि बलवान् ॥ ७६ ॥

76. It is a great pity that the wicked trunkless Rahu, dark, from sin, and of unknown abode, verily devours the glowing sun, who with his thousand dazzling rays overspreads the earth. Who indeed is (more) powerful (than) the operative age-Karma when the time (of its cessation) arrives.

**Commentary.**

The mythological belief in Indian astronomy with regard to the phenomenon of the solar eclipse is that at fixed periods of time the Sun inspite of his brilliary power and beauty and grandeur is subject to being swallowed by the planet Rahu which is believed to be a mere head without a trunk, of dark complexion, and of low and unknown origin. In the same way when the age-Karma has worked out, and Death comes, all power and glory, is of no avail. Herein Death is compared to Rahu, and Soul to the Sun. The moral is that Death is inevitable, and therefore one must not delay, but must expedite the adoption of right conduct for eternal bliss.

उत्पाद्य मोहमदविह्वलमेव विश्वं
वेधाः स्वयं गतघृणष्ठगवद्यथेष्टम् ।
संसारभीकरमहागहनान्तराले
हन्ता निवारयितुमत्र हि कः समर्थः ॥ ७७ ॥

77. What brave person (literally Killer) is capable of counteracting the cruel Karma who alone has distressed all (mundane souls) with intoxication and delusion just as he pleased, like a thug, in this frightful and dense forest of the world.

कदा कथं कुतः कस्मिन्नित्यतर्क्यः खलोऽन्तकः ।
प्राप्नोत्येव किमित्याध्वं यतध्वं श्रेयसे बुधाः ॥ ७८ ॥

78. Wicked death is certainly overtaking all; it cannot be guessed as to when, how, whence, for whom, and in which way (it comes). Let all wise men look to their welfare.

असामवायिकं मृत्योरेकमालोक्य कञ्चन ।
देशं कालं विधिं हेतुं निश्चिन्ताः सन्तु जन्तवः ॥ ७९ ॥

79. May all living beings be free from anxiety on seeing that Death is sudden and has no (fixed) place, time, mode, and cause.

अपिहितमहाघोरद्वारं न किं नरकापदा-
मुपकृतवतो भूयः किं तेन चेदमपाकरोत् ।
कुशलविलयज्वालाजाले कलत्रकलेवरे
कथमिव भवानत्र प्रीतः पृथग्जनदुर्लभे ॥ ८० ॥

80. Why are you attached to the body of women, which is difficult of acquisition by every man, which is like a net of flames, destroying welfare. Is it (body) not an open and terrible gate to the miseries of hell? Of what use is it to thee? It has wronged (you), who have often done it good (nourished it).

व्यापत्पर्वमयं विरामविरसं मूलेऽप्यभोग्योचितं
विष्वक्क्षुत्क्षतपातकुष्टकुथिताद्युग्रामयैः छिद्रितम् ।
मानुष्यं घुणभक्षितेक्षुसदृशं नाम्नैकरम्यं पुन-
र्निःसारं परलोकबीजमचिरात्कृत्वेह सारीकुरु ॥ ८१ ॥

81. As a sugarcane eaten up by *Ghuna* worms, (is) full of joints (at intervals), tasteless at the (outer) end,

uneatable at the root, sweet in name, but having no pulp, so the human body (is full of) calamities at intervals (insipid in old age, unenjoyable in infancy), and throughout injured by frightful diseases like hunger, wounds, leprosy, laceration, etc., (good looking in name only, but of no utility). (If such a piece of sugarcane is sowed in the ground, it produces many fruits. Similarly you should) make (this body) here useful without any delay, by making it a seed (to produce, good in) the next world.

प्रसुप्तो मरणाशङ्कां प्रबुद्धो जीवितोत्सवम् ।
प्रत्यहं जनयत्येष तिष्ठेत्काये कियच्चिरम् ॥ ८२ ॥

82. Every day while sleeping, he wears the appearance of death and while awaking he makes merry on his being alive. Every day produces this (scene). How long can this soul live in the body.

सत्यं वदात्र यदि जन्मनि बन्धुकृत्य-
माप्तं त्वया किमपि बन्धुजनाद्धितार्थम् ।
एतावदेव परमस्ति मृतस्य पश्चात्
संभूय कायमहितं तव भस्मयन्ति ॥ ८३ ॥

83. Say truly if in this life any act whatsoever of fraternal nature has been done thee by thy relatives, for thy good. This is the only good, that after (thy) death having assembled together, (they) cremate thy body, which is (thy) enemy.

जन्मसन्तानसम्पादिविवाहादिविधायिनः ।
स्वाः परेऽस्य सकृत्प्राणहारिणो न परे परे ॥ ८४ ॥

84. One's relatives, who arrange marriage, etc., which cause a series of births are the enemies of the soul. The others who take away life only once, are not enemies.

**Commentary.**

Family members involve a person in the meshes of delusion, and make his spiritual advancement impossible, and thus ruin the future. An enemy only kills the body once, but family members ruin many future lives of the Soul.

रे धनेन्धनसंभारं प्रक्षिप्याशाहुताशने ।
ज्वलन्तं मन्यते भ्रान्तः शान्तं संधुक्षणे क्षणे ॥ ८५ ॥

85. What a deluded soul it is who having fed the fire of desire with the faggot of wealth, (*i. e.*, worldly objects, and himself) burning (in it) considers himself refreshed while he is blowing (the fire) every moment.

पलितच्छलेन देहान् निर्गच्छति शुद्धिरेव तव बुद्धेः ।
कथमिव परलोकार्थं जरी वराकस्तदा स्मरति ॥ ८६ ॥

86. Under the pretence of grey hair, the (essence or) purity of thy wisdom goes out of the body; how can a wretched old man remember at that age (his duty) for the next world ?

इष्टार्थाद्यदवाप्ततद्भवसुखक्षाराम्भसि प्रस्फुर-
न्नानामानसदुःखवाडवशिखासंदीपिताभ्यन्तरे ।
मृत्यूत्पत्तिजरातरंगचपले संसारघोरार्णवे ।
मोहग्राहविदारितास्यविवराद्दूरेचरा दुर्लभाः ॥ ८७ ॥

87. It is difficult to find men, who keep at a distance from the wide gaping mouth of the alligator of Delusion in the vast ocean of Samsára, full of salt water of worldly enjoyments (incapable of quenching the thirst), produced by desired objects. (The) heart (of Samsára) is inflamed by various kinds of excruciating mental sufferings which are burning like the flame of the sub-marine fire (Barawá-nala) and is disturbed by the waves of birth, old age, and death.

अव्युच्छिन्नैः सुखपरिकरैर्लालिता लोलरम्यैः
श्यामांगीनां नयनकमलैरार्चिता यौवनान्तम् ।
धन्योऽसि त्वं यदि तनुरियं लब्धबोधे मृगीभि-
र्दग्धारण्यस्थलकमलिनीशङ्कयालोक्यते ते ॥ ८८ ॥

88. If this body of thine which has, in the full bloom of thy youth, been nourished by a continuous series of

enjoyments, and adored by beautiful women with lotus eyes charming in their agility, is on acquisition of discrimination (subjected to such austerities in the forest) that the she-deer takes thee for a land-lotus in a burnt down wood, then all praise be to thee.

बाल्ये वेत्सि न किञ्चिदप्यपरिपूर्णांगो हितं वाहिते
कामान्धः खलु कामिनी द्रुमघन भ्राम्यन्वने यौवने ।
मध्ये वृद्धतृषार्ज्जितुं वसुपशुः क्लिश्नासि कृष्यादिभि-
र्वृद्धो वार्द्धमृतः क जन्मफलिते धर्मो भवेन्निर्मलः ॥ ८९ ॥

89. In thy boyhood, when thy body is immature, thou dost not know anything whatsoever as to thy benefit or harm; in thy youth, blinded by sex-passion, thou, ramblest in a forest, dense with trees in the form of women; in thy middle age, thou sufferest because of thy great greed; like a loaded beast, by agriculture, etc., pursued to earn (money), and in thy old age, thou art as if half-dead. Which, then, (is the age) when life should bear fruit in pure Dharma.

बाल्येऽस्मिन् यदनेन ते विरचितं स्मर्त्तुं च तन्नोचितं
मध्ये चापि धनार्ज्जनव्यतिकरैस्तन्नार्पितं यत्त्वयि ।
वार्द्धक्येऽप्यभिभूय दन्तदलनाद्यचेष्टितं निष्ठुरम्
पश्याद्यापि विधेर्वशेन चलितुं वाञ्छस्यहो दुर्म्मते ॥ ९० ॥

90. In thy boyhood whatsoever is done by thee is not fit even to be remembered; in thy middle age there is no (pain) that is not given to thee by the troubles of acquiring riches; (and) even in thy old age (thou seest) the (Karma's) cruel act of despising thee by rooting out thy teeth. Oh fool, See, dost thou still wish to live under the control of Karma.

अश्रोत्रीव तिरस्कृता परतिरस्कारश्रुतीनां श्रुतिः
चक्षुर्वीक्षितुमक्षमं तव दशां दूष्यामि वान्ध्यं गतम् ।

भीत्येवाभिमुखान्तकादतितरां कायोऽप्ययं कम्पते
निष्कम्पस्त्वमहो प्रदीप्तभवनेऽप्यास्स जराजर्ज्जरे ॥ ९१ ॥

91. Thy out-raged ear has turned deaf as if not to hear the offending words of others; thy eyes have gone blind as if to disable thee from seeing thy consurable condition ; thy body trembles greatly as if out of fear of death, which stares thee in thy face ; it is a great wonder that thou art still sitting inactive (in thy body) which is worn out by old age, (and which is crumbling like) a house on fire.

अतिपरिचितेष्ववज्ञा नवे भवेत् प्रीतिरिति हि जनवादः ।
त्वं किमिति मृषा कुरुषे दोषासक्तो गुणेष्वरतः ॥ ९२ ॥

92. It is said by people that familiarity breeds contempt, and love for a new object attracts, why (then) dost thou falsify this (proverb) by infatuation for wrong (belief, etc.,) and aversion to right (belief, etc.).

हंसैर्न भुक्तमतिकर्कशमम्भसापि
नो संगतं दिनविकाशि सरोजमित्थम् ।
नालोकितं मधुकरेण मृतं वृथैव
प्रायः कुतो व्यसनिनो स्वहिते विवेकः ॥ ९३ ॥

93. The bee, (which) did not see that the day-blooming lotus, being too hard (in stalk) was neither enjoyed by the geese, nor befriended by water (as it remained apart from it), died in vain, (by being enamoured of the lotus, and getting suffocated within it when it closed at night). How can there generally be discrimination for one's good in the sensualist ?

प्रज्ञैव दुर्लभा सुष्ठु दुर्लभा सान्यजन्मनि ।
तां प्राप्य ये प्रमाद्यन्ति ते शोच्याः खलु धीमताम् ॥ ९४ ॥

94. Indeed it is difficult to acquire wisdom. It is much more difficult (to live so as) to have it in the next life, verily, by the wise are to be pitied, those, who having

acquired that (wisdom) here, are careless (of spiritual advancement).

लोकाधिपाः क्षितिभुजो भुवि येन जाता-
स्तस्मिन् विधौ सति हि सर्वजनप्रसिद्धे ।
शोच्यं तदेव यदमी स्पृहणीयवीर्य्या-
स्तेषां बुधाश्च वत किङ्करतां प्रयान्ति ॥ ९५ ॥

95. Even while (right-conduct), renowned among all people, by which (men) became sovereigns, and enjoyers of earth, can be followed, it is a pity that these wise men possessed of enviable might, accept the service of such (sovereigns, and do not practise that right-conduct),

यस्मिन्नस्ति स भूभृतो धृतमहावंशाः प्रदेशः परः
प्रज्ञापारमिताधृतोन्नतिखना मूर्द्धना ध्रियन्ते श्रियै ।
भूयांस्तस्य भुजङ्गदुर्गमतमो मार्गो निराशस्ततो
व्यक्तं वक्तुमयुक्तमार्य्यमहतां सर्वार्य्यसाक्षात्कृतः ॥ ९६ ॥

96. That religion is the best, by (having followed) which (there were born) monarchs of very high families, who reached the height of wisdom, and acquired great prosperity; and to whom were bowed the heads of (persons) desirous of wealth. The great path of that (religion) which is very difficult of access to the voluptuous and is free from desires, cannot properly be described by even the greatest of saints, and was only proclaimed by the omniscient.

शरीरेऽस्मिन् सर्वाशुचिनि बहुदुःखेऽपि निवसन्
व्यरंसीन्नो नैव प्रथयति जनः प्रीतिमधिकाम् ।
इमं दृष्ट्वाप्यस्माद्विरमयितुमेनं च यतते
यतिर्याताख्यानैः परहितरतिं पश्य महतः ॥ ९७ ॥

97. A person living in this all-impure and very painful body does not become averse to it, (but) becomes greatly attached to it. A saint knowing this tries to

dissuade him from this with admonitions. See a high-minded person's love of doing good to others.

इत्थं तथेति बहुना किमुदीरितेन
भूयस्त्वयैव ननु जन्मनि भुक्तमुक्तम् ।
एतावदेव कथितं तव संकलय्य
सर्वापदां पदमिदं जननं जनानाम् ॥ ९८ ॥

98. Of what avail is it to point out repeatedly that this (body) is such, *i. e.*, full of miseries and troubles and impurities.) Verily thou thyself hast enjoyed and discarded (it) in various births. Briefly this much alone is said to thee that this body is the abode of all miseries for living beings.

अन्तर्वातं वदनविवरे क्षुत्तृषार्त्तः प्रतीच्छन्
कर्म्मायत्तः सुचिरमुदरावस्करे वृद्धगृद्ध्या ।
निष्पन्दात्मा कृमिसहचरो जन्मनि क्लेशभीतो
मन्ये जन्मिन्नपि च मरणात्तन्निमित्ताद्बिभेषि ॥ ९९ ॥

99. Under the sway of Karma, oppressed by hunger and thirst, thou hast while in the filthy womb, under the greed of growing, long desired to have in the hole of thy mouth what was eaten (by thy mother). Thou didst befriend the worms (there) and wast motionless being afraid of the pain in being born. Oh! born one. I think thou art (for the same reason) also afraid of death the cause of (birth).

अजाकृपाणीयमनुष्ठितं त्वया विकल्पमुग्धेन भवादितः पुरा ।
यदत्र किञ्चित्सुखरूपमाप्यते तदार्य विद्ध्यन्धकवर्त्तकीयकम् ॥

100. From the very beginning of birth, being devoid of discrimination thou hast played the part of the goat (who dug out) the knife (by which he was killed). Oh simple one, know that whatever trivial happiness is to be had here is like a blind man's accidently catching a sparrow.

हा कष्टमिष्टवनिताभिरकाण्ड एव
विखण्डयति पण्डितमानिनोऽपि ।

पश्यादूभुतं तदपि घोरतया सहन्ते
दग्धुं तपोऽग्निभिरमुं न समुत्सहन्ते ॥ १०१ ॥

**101.** It is a pity, that cupid unexpectedly, worries through lovely women even those who consider themselves to be wise. See the wonder then, that they suffer deeply, but do not make bold to burn it by the fire of austerities.

अर्थिभ्यस्तृणवद्विचिन्त्य विषयान् कश्चिच्छ्रियं दत्तवान्
पापां तामवितर्पिणीं विगणयन्नादात्परस्त्यक्तवान् ।
प्रागेवाकुशलां विमृश्य सुभगोऽप्यन्यो न पर्यग्रही-
द्देते ते विदितोत्तरोत्तरवराः सर्वोत्तमास्त्यागिनः ॥ १०२ ॥

**102.** Considering the objects of desire like straw, one gave his wealth to those who needed it; another, thinking it to be sinful and cause of discontent abandodned it at the outset; and another good person did not accept it from the very first, thinking it to be evil. Know that each one of these (three) high renouncers is better than the preceding one.

विरज्य सम्पदः सन्तस्त्यजन्ति किमिहाद्भुतम् ।
मावमीत्किं जुगुप्सावान् सुभुक्तमपि भोजनम् ॥ १०३ ॥

**103.** What wonder is there that men leave their fortune, after being disgusted with it? Does not one vomit even well-taken food on feeling disgusted with it?

श्रियं त्यजन् जड शोकं विस्मयं सात्विकं सताम् ।
करोति तत्त्वविच्चित्रं न शोकं न च विस्मयम् ॥ १०४॥

**104.** A fool feels sorry and a brave man proud in discarding fortune. It is a marvel that one, who knows the real nature of (wordly objects) feels neither sorry nor proud (in doing so).

विमृश्योच्चैर्गर्भात् प्रभृति मृतिपर्यन्तमखिलम्
मुधाप्येतत् क्लेशाशुचिभयनिकाराघबहुलम् ।

बुधैस्त्याज्यं त्यागाद्यदि भवति मुक्तिश्च जडधी
स कस्त्यक्तुं नालं खलजनसमायोगसदृशम् ॥ १०५ ।

105. Knowing well this (body) from its conception all along to its death to be full of pain, filthiness, fear, contempt, and sin, and also of no avail, it is fit to be abandoned by the wise, if by abandonment liberation can be had. What fool is that who cannot give up this body, as (injurious as) the company of a wicked man.

कुबोधरागादिविचेष्टितैः फलम्
त्वयापि भूयोजननादि लक्षणम् ।
प्रतीहि भव्यप्रतिलोमवर्त्तिभि-
र्ध्रुवं फलं प्राप्स्यसि तद्विलक्षणम् ॥१०६॥

106. Thou hast suffered the consequence of false knowledge, attachment and such evil acts, in the shape of births and re-births. Be assured that thou wilt certainly attain just the opposite result (*i. e.* liberation) by noble acts of an opposite character (absence of attatchment, etc.).

दयादमत्यागसमाधिसन्ततेः पथि प्रयाहि प्रगुणं प्रयत्नवान् ।
नयत्यवश्यं वचसामगोचरं विकल्पदूरं परमं किमप्यसौ ॥१०७॥

107. Pursue actively and straight, the path of continuous observance of compassion, self-control, renunciation, and equanimity. This verily leads (thee) to the highest (position), free from anxieties and beyond the power of words (to describe).

विज्ञाननिहितमोहं कुटीप्रवेशो विशुद्धकायमिव ।
त्यागः परिग्रहाणामवश्यमजरामरं कुरुते ॥१०८॥

108. The renunciation of mundane objects undoubtedly liberates one who has shaken off delusion by means of right-knowledge, from decrepitude and death; just as *Kuti Pravesha* (a kind of austerity) makes the body pure.

अभुक्त्वापि परित्यागात्स्वोच्छिष्टं विश्वमासितम् ।
येनचित्रं नमस्तस्मै कुमारब्रह्मचारिणे ॥१०९॥

**109.** Obeisance to that young celibate, to whom the whole world, having been renounced without being enjoyed, is curiously, a remnant (of his past enjoyments).

अकिञ्चनोऽहमित्यास्स्व त्रैलोक्याधिपतिर्भवेः ।
योगिगम्यं तव प्रोक्तं रहस्यं परमात्मनः ॥११०॥

**110.** Live in a way as though (you felt), "Nothing is mine" and thou wilt be lord over the three worlds. The essence of divinity, as realised by the saints, is told thee (herein.)

दुर्लभमशुद्धमपसुखमविदितमृतिसमयमल्पपरमायुः ।
मानुष्यमिहैव तपो मुक्तिस्तपसैव तत्तपः कार्यम् ॥१११॥

**111.** It is difficult to obtain this human life, which is impure, and void of happiness, the death time of which is not known, and which is of very short duration. Austerity can be practised in this human life; and Liberation can be obtained only through austerities. Hence austerity should be practised.

आराध्यो भगवान् जगत्त्रयगुरुर्वृत्तिः सतां सम्मता
क्लेशस्तच्चरणस्मृतिः क्षतिरपि प्रप्रक्षयः कर्मणाम् ।
साध्यं सिद्धिसुखं कियान् परिमितः कालो मनःसाधनम्
सम्यक् चेतसि चिन्तयन्तु विधुरं किं वा समाधौ बुधाः ११२

**112.** The one to be propitiated is the Lord, the preceptor of the three worlds. The course of life is to be one applauded by the good. The only trouble is to remember the conduct of that (Lord). The only loss is the wasting away of Karmas. The goal to be achieved is the bliss of Liberation. The Time (required) is limited. Mind only is to be controlled. Let the wise think rightly in their mind, what difficulty is there in realization of the self.

द्रविणपवनप्राध्मातानां सुखं किमिहेक्षते
किमपि किमयं कामव्याधः खलीकुरुते खलः ।

चरणमपि किं स्पृष्टुं शक्ताः पराभवपांशवो
वदत तपसोऽप्यन्यन्मान्यं समीहितसाधनम् ॥११३॥

**113**. What happiness does (a man) see in those who are oppressed by the hot winds of wealth. Can this wicked Desire, hunter-like, spoil (the character of a good man)? Can the dust of humiliation even touch the feet (of an ascetic)? Tell me, if there be any other laudable means except asceticism, of attaining (liberation).

इहैव सहजान् रिपून्विजयते प्रकोपादिकान्
गुणाः परिणमन्ति यानसुभिरप्ययं वाञ्छति ।
पुरश्च पुरुषार्थसिद्धिरचिरात् स्वयं यायिनी
नरो न रमते कथं तपसि तापसंहारिणी ॥११४॥

**114**. In this very (world, the ascetic) vanquishes (his) enemies, anger and other (passions), and acquires merits which (one) wishes for even by (laying down one's) life. The success of human efforts (Liberation) comes in front, of itself. Why does not a man then take delight in austerity, the annihilator of pain.

तपोऽवल्यां देहः समुपचितपुण्यार्जितफलः
शलाट्वग्रे यस्य प्रसव इव कालेन गलितः ।
व्यशुष्यच्चायुष्यं सलिलमिव संरक्षितपयः
स धन्यः संन्यासाहुतभुजि समाधानचरमम् ॥११५॥

**115**. Blessed is he whose body drops down like the flower at the end of an unripe fruit, after having produced the full grown fruit of merit in the creeper of austerity; and whose (stream of) life, (having attained) complete self-realization is dried up in the fire of asceticism, like water protecting milk.

अमी प्ररूढवैराग्यास्तनुमप्यनुपाल्य यत् ।
तपस्यन्ति चिरं तद्धि ज्ञातं ज्ञानस्य वैभवम् ॥११६॥

**116**. Know this as the glory of knowledge that these spritually-advanced ascetics practise austerities for long, and take care of the body also.

क्षणार्द्धमपि देहेन साहचर्य्यं सहेत कः ।
यदि प्रकोष्ठमादाय न स्याद्बोधो निरोधकः ॥११७॥

**117.** What ascetic would have suffered association with this body even for half a moment, if Right Knowledge had not by grasping his wrist prevented him (from getting rid of it)?

समस्तं साम्राज्यं तृणमिव परित्यज्य भगवा-
न्तपस्यन्निर्म्माणः क्षुधित इव दीनः परगृहान् ।
किलाटेद्भिक्षार्थी स्वयमलभमानोऽपि सुचिरं
न सोढव्यं किं वा परमिह परैः कार्यवशतः ॥११८॥

**118.** Verily did the Lord (Rishabha Deva) himself, after renouncing all his empire, like a straw, and being engaged in austerities, wander without pride, for food, like a poor hungry person, to the door of others, and did not get it for a long time. What difficulties should others not endure for the sake of their object (of obtaining liberation)?

पुरा गर्भादिन्द्रो मुकुलितकरः किङ्कर इव
स्वयं स्रष्टा सृष्टेः पतिरथनिधीनां निजसुतः ।
क्षुधित्वा षण्मासान् स किल पुरुरप्याट जगती-
महो केनाप्यस्मिन् विलसितमलंघ्यं हतविधेः ॥११९॥

**119.** Whom (for 6 month) before conception Indra (served) with folded hands, like a servant, who himself (was) the organiser of all organisation, whose son (Bharata was) the possesser of the (nine) treasures (Nidhis), even he, the great (Rishabha Deva) wandered on earth for 6 months, without getting food. Well, the frolics of Doomed Destiny (Karma) are insurmountable by anyone.

प्राक् प्रकाशप्रधानः स्यात् प्रदीप इव संयमी ।
पश्चात्तापप्रकाशाभ्यां भास्वानिव हि भासताम् ॥१२०॥

**120.** An ascetic, in the first stage chiefly radiates light (of knowledge), like a lamp. Later on he glows with light and glory (of omniscience) like the sun.

भूत्वा दीपोपमो धीमान् ज्ञानचारित्रभास्वरः ।
स्वमन्यं भासयत्येष प्रोद्वमत्कर्मकज्जलम् ॥१२१॥

121. The wise (ascetic) who resembles a lamp, becomes resplendent with right-knowledge and right conduct, and removing the soot of Karmas, makes the self and non-self manifest.

अशुभाच्छुभमायातः शुद्धः स्यादयमागमात् ।
रवेरप्राप्तसन्ध्यस्य तमसो न समुद्गमः ॥१२२॥

122. Emerging from evil into good, this (soul) reaches, with the help of the scriptures, (the stage of) pure thought activity. Darkness (of ignorance) cannot exist in presence of the pre-evening sun (of knowledge).

विधूततमसो रागस्तपःश्रुतनिबन्धनः ।
संध्याराग इवार्कस्य जन्तोरभ्युदयाय सः ॥१२३॥

123. The red tinge (*i.e.*, attachment), of a person whose ignorance is dispelled, supports austerity and scriptural knowledge; and like the red dawn of the rising sun is for the prosperity of all beings.

विहाय व्याप्तमालोकं पुरस्कृत्य पुनस्तमः ।
रविवद्रागमागच्छन् पातालतलमृच्छति ॥१२४॥

124. But, one having attachment (otherwise) goes down below like the (setting) sun, leaving the spreading light and plunging forward into darkness.

ज्ञानं यत्र पुरःसरं सहचरी लज्जा तपः संवलम्
चारित्रं शिविका निवेशनभुवः स्वर्गा गुणा रक्षकाः ।
पंथाश्च प्रगुणं शमाम्बुबहुलः छाया दया भावना
यानं तन्मुनिमापयेदभिमतं स्थानं विना विप्लवैः ॥१२५॥

125. Such a passage of meditation would lead an ascetic to the desired goal, without any mishaps, where knowledge is the guide, modesty a companion, austerities the provision, right conduct a palanquin, heavens the

halting places, merits guards, the way straight, with abundance of the water of tranquility (of mind), compassion a shade, and meditation a chariot.

मिथ्या दृष्टिविषान्वदन्ति फणिनो दृष्टं तदा सुस्फुटं
यासामर्द्धविलोकनैरपि जगद्दन्दह्यते सर्वतः ।
तास्त्वय्येव विलोमवर्त्तिनि भृशं भ्राम्यन्ति बद्धक्रुधः
स्त्रीरूपेण विषं हि केवलमतस्तद्गोचरं मास्मगाः ॥१२६॥

126. They wrongly call cobras to be poisonous by sight, when it has been clearly seen, that even by half a glance of (women) the world is wholly burnt out. When thou hast turned away from them, they roam about thee in anger. The only poison is the woman. Do not therefore approach the same.

क्रुद्धाः प्राणहरा भवन्ति भुजगा दष्ट्वैव काले क्वचि-
त्तेषामौषधयश्च सन्ति बहवः सद्योविषव्युच्छिदः ।
हन्युः स्त्रीभुजगाः पुरेह च मुहुः क्रुद्धाः प्रसन्नास्तथा
योगीन्द्रानपि तान्निरौषधविषा दृष्टाश्च दृष्ट्वापि च ॥१२७॥

127. Cobras are deprivers of life, only occasionally when they bite in rage, there are many remedies which quickly remove their poison. Women-cobras whether in rage or in smiles, kill even master-ascetics, here and hereafter, again and again, whether they bite, or are looked at; and by looking or being looked at, and there is no remedy for their poison.

एतामुत्तमनायिकामभिजनावर्ज्यां जगत्प्रेयसीं
मुक्तिश्रीललनां गुणप्रणयिनीं गन्तुं तवेच्छा यदि ।
तां त्वं संस्कुरु वर्जयान्यवनिता वार्त्तामपि प्रस्फुटं
तस्यामेव रतिं तनुष्व नितरां प्रायेण सेर्ष्याः स्त्रियः ॥१२८॥

128. If thou desirest to have this exquisite and beautiful woman, eternal bliss, inaccessible to men of common run, dear to the whole world and a lover of virtues, then adorn her; give up entirely the talk of any other woman;

(and) show your love constantly to her alone ; (since) women, as a rule, are jealous.

वचनसलिलैर्हासस्वच्छैस्तरङ्गसुखोदरै-
र्वदनकमलैर्बाह्येरम्याः स्त्रियः सरसीसमाः ।
इह हि बहवः प्रास्तप्रज्ञास्तटेऽपि पिपासवो
विषयविषमग्राहग्रस्ताः पुनर्न समुद्गताः ॥१२९॥

**129.** Women are like lakes, outwardly inviting; their talk, and laughter, are pleasant like clear water with waves, their faces are like lotuses. On their banks only, many foolish and thirsty (men) have been caught by the terrible crocodile of Desire and have never emerged.

पापिष्ठैर्जगती विधीतमभितः प्रज्वाल्य रागानलं
क्रुद्धैरिन्द्रियलुब्धकैर्भयपदैः संत्रासिता सर्वतः ।
हन्तैते शरणैषिणो जनमृगाः स्त्रीछद्मना निर्म्मितम्
घातस्थानमुपाश्रयन्ति मदनव्याधाधिपस्याकुलाः ॥१३०॥

**130.** How sad it is that men like deer desiring for shelter, enter the slaughter-house of Cupid, the master-hunter, constructed in the form of women, when the world is frightened on all sides by the enraged, terror-striking, and wicked sense-gratification hunters, who have made and kindled the fire of desire all around.

अपत्रप तपोऽग्निना भयजुगुप्सयोरास्पदं
शरीरमिदमर्द्धदग्धशववन्न किं पश्यसि ।
वृथा व्रजसि किं रतिं ननु न भीषयस्यातुरो
निसर्गतरलाः स्त्रियस्त्वदिह ताः स्फुटं बिभ्यति ॥१३१॥

**131.** Oh shameless (ascetic)! Dost thou not see this body (of thine), rendered, by the fire of austerity, an object of contempt and fear, like a half-burnt corpse. Afflicted by desire, why dost thou entertain vain love, and not frighten them ; The naturally tremulous women however, are evidently afraid of thee.

Verses **132, 133, 134** omitted.

कण्ठस्थः कालकूटोऽपि शम्भोः किमपि नाकरोत्।
सोऽपि दन्दह्यते स्त्रीभिः स्त्रियो हि विषमं विषम् ॥१३५॥

135. Even Shiva, who was not at all effected by the deadly poison in his throat, was affected by women. Women indeed are the worst of poisons.

तव युवतिशरीरे सर्वदोषैकपात्रे
रतिरमृतमयूखाद्यर्थसाधर्म्यतश्चेत्।
ननु शुचिषु शुभेषु प्रीतिरेष्वेव साध्वी
मदनमधुमदान्धे प्रायशः को विवेकः ॥१३६॥

136. Thy attachment for the woman's body, which is full of defects, is because of its resemblance with the moon, etc. Verily the attachment for these good and pure (objects) is praise-worthy. (But) what discrimination can, there be in a man blinded by the intoxication of the wine of lust.

प्रियामनुभवत्स्वयं भवति कातरं केवलं
परेष्वनुभवत्सु तां विषयिषु स्फुटं ह्लादते।
मनो ननु नपुंसकं त्विति न शब्दतश्चार्थतः
सुधी कथमनेन सन्नुभयथा पुमान् जीयते ॥१३७॥

137. The mind itself is totally impotent in enjoying the beloved, (and) rejoices greatly while others (the senses) are enjoying her. The mind is neuter not only in grammar but in sense also. Why (then) is the wise man, who is both ways (grammatically and practically) masculine, be vanquished by mind?

राज्यं सौजन्ययुक्तं श्रुतवदुरुतपः पूज्यमत्रापि यस्मात्
त्यक्त्वा राज्यं तपस्यन्नलघुरतिलघुः स्यात्तपः प्रोह्य राज्यम्।
राज्यात्तस्मात्प्रपूज्यं तप इति मनसाऽऽलोच्य धीमानुदग्रं
कुर्यादार्यः समग्रं प्रभवभयहरं सत्तपः पापभीरुः ॥१३८॥

138. In this world sovereignty with just rule and with scriptural knowledge is respected as a high austerity. Since one relinquishing sovereignty and practising austerity

is great, and the one relinquishing austerity and taking up sovereignty is very low, therefore asceticism is superior to kingship. Thinking thus, a sin-fearing, noble, and wise man, should whole-heartedly practise the exalted noble austerity which removes all fear of transmigration.

पुरा शिरसि धार्यन्ते पुष्पाणि विबुधैरपि ।
पश्चात्पादोऽपि नास्प्राक्षीत्किं न कुर्याद्गुणच्युतिः ॥१३९॥

139. Flowers are first placed even by celestials on their heads, afterwards (when the fragrance has died out) even the foot does not touch them. What may not result from a loss of merits?

हे चन्द्रमः किमिति लाञ्छनवानभूस्त्वम्
तद्वान् भवेः किमिति तन्मय एव नाभूः ।
किं ज्योत्स्नया मलमलं तव घोषयन्त्या
स्वर्भानुवन्ननु तथा सति नासि लक्ष्यः ॥१४०॥

140. Oh! moon why art thou with a spot. If thou hast it, why art thou not all one with it? What is the good of thy light, which clearly proclaims (thy) blemish? Verily thou wouldst not have been the butt if thou hadst been (all black) like the planet Rahu.

विकाशयन्ति भव्यस्य मनोमुकुलमंशवः
रवेरिवारविन्दस्य कठोराश्च गुरूक्तयः ॥१४१॥

141. Even the harsh words of a preceptor open the bud of the heart of one, fit to be liberated, just as the rays of the sun (do) blossom a lotus bud.

दोषान्कांश्चन तान्प्रवर्त्तकतया प्रच्छाद्य गच्छत्ययं
सार्द्धं तैः सहसा म्रियेद्यदि गुरुः पश्चात् करोत्येष किम् ।
तस्मान्मे न गुरुर्गुरुर्गुरुतरान् कृत्वा लघूंश्च स्फुटम्
ब्रूते यः सततं समीक्ष्य निपुणं सोऽयं खलः सद्गुरुः ॥१४२॥

142. If a preceptor over-looks several faults of a pupil, with a view to set them right (afterwards), and if the pupil suddenly dies with them, then what can that

(Guru) do? Hence that preceptor is not my preceptor, who makes little of my faults ; (but) that wicked man is a true preceptor, who observes my defects in details, and proclaims them constantly.

लोकद्वयहितं वक्तुं श्रोतुं च सुलभाः पुरा ।
दुर्लभाः कर्तुमद्यत्वे वक्तुं श्रोतुं च दुर्लभाः ॥१४३॥

**143.** Formerly it was easy to find speakers and hearers of words, useful for both the worlds, but men who acted up to them were scarce. But now-a-days (even) the speakers and hearers (of wholesome words) are rare.

गुणागुणविवेकिभिर्विहितमप्यलं दूषणं
भवेत्सदुपदेशवन्मतिमतामतिप्रीतये ।
कृतं किमपि धार्ष्ट्यतः स्तवनमप्यतीर्थोषितै-
र्न तोषयति तन्मनांसि खलु कष्टमज्ञानता ॥१४४॥

**144.** To the wise, even the faults found by the discriminators between virtue and vice, are a cause of great pleasure, like wholesome advice. (And) even irrelevant praise by the vicious, does not gratify their hearts. Ignorance is surely to be pitied.

त्यक्तहेत्वन्तरापेक्षौ गुणदोषनिबन्धनौ ।
यस्यादानपरित्यागौ स एव विदुषां वरः ॥१४५॥

**145.** Only he whose acceptance and renunciation are associated with merits and demerits (respectively), independently of any other consideration, is the wise of the wise.

हितं हित्वाहिते स्थित्वा दुर्धीर्दुःखायसे भृशम् ।
विपर्यये तयोरेधि त्वं सुखायिष्यसे सुधीः ॥१४६॥

**146.** By abandoning the beneficial and by adopting the injurious (path), a fool suffers seriously. Proceed on the contrary (path), and thou wilt be happy, O wise man. Attachment even to wholesome things must be given up.

इमे दोषास्तेषां प्रभवनममीभ्यो नियमितो
गुणाश्चैते तेषामपि भवनमेतेभ्य इति यः ।

स्यजंस्त्याज्यान् हेतून् झटिति हितहेतून् प्रतिभजन्
स विद्वान् सद्वृत्तः स हि स हि निधिः सौख्ययशसोः ॥१४७॥

147. One, who has ascertained that these are demerits and these are their origins, and that these are merits and from these they have sprung, promptly abandons and accepts the objects (respectively), worthy of abandonment and acceptance. Such a one is wise, such a one is along the right line of conduct, and only such a one is a repository of bliss and renown.

साधारणौ सकलजन्तुषु वृद्धिनाशौ
जन्मान्तरार्जितशुभाशुभकर्मयोगात् ।
धीमान्स यः सुगतिसाधनवृद्धिनाश-
स्तद्व्यत्ययाद्विगतधीरपरोऽभ्यधायि ॥१४८॥

148. Rise and fall are common to all things according to the meritorious and demeritorious Karmas acquired in past life. That man is wise who for attaining a good next condition of existence increases (his merits), and removes his (demerits). The man opposed to this (view) is a fool. This has been said.

कलौ दण्डो नीतिः स च नृपतिभिस्ते नृपतयो
नयन्त्यर्थार्थं तं न च धनमदोऽस्त्याश्रमवताम् ।
नतानामाचार्या न हि नतिरताः साधुचरिता-
स्तपस्तेषु श्रीमन्मणय इव जाताः प्रविरलाः ॥ १४९ ॥

149. In this Kali age, justice is by punishment, and it (is awarded) by the Kings. The Kings employ it to exact money. The ascetics have no pride of money. The preceptors are fond of obeisance and are only led by those who bow to them. Among ascetics, those who follow right conduct and are not fond of obeisance are scarce like resplendent gems.

एते ते मुनिमानिनः कवलिताः कान्ताकटाक्षेक्षणै-
रङ्गालग्नशरावसन्नहरिणप्रख्या भ्रमन्त्याकुलाः ।

सन्धत्तुं विषयाटवीस्थलतले स्वान्क्वाप्यहो न क्षमाः
मात्राजीन्मरुदाहताभ्रचपलैः संसर्गमेभिर्भवान् ॥१५०॥

150. Those, who call themselves ascetics, are a prey to the side-long glances of the eyes of women. Like deer with their bodies pierced by arrows, they wander distressed. Alas! they are not able to rest themselves any where on the face of the earth in this forest of desire. O you, do not come in contact with (such saints) who are fickle like the clouds, beaten by winds.

गेहं गुहा परिदधासि दिशो विहाय-
संयानमिष्टमशनं तपसोऽभिवृद्धिः ।
प्राप्तागमार्थं तव सन्ति गुणाः कलत्र-
मप्रार्थ्यवृत्तिरसि यासि वृथैव याञ्चाम् ॥१५१॥

151. Thy residence is a cave; thou art clad with the points of the compass; the sky is thy vehicle; advancement in austerities is (thy) palatable meal, (and) the qualities (of a saint) thy beloved wife. Thy food is free from humble supplication. In vain dost thou, O acquirer of the essence of the scriptures, become a supplicant (for worldly objects).

परमाणोः परं नाल्पं नभसो न महत्परम् ।
इति ब्रुवन् किमद्राक्षीन्निमौ दीनाभिमानिनौ ॥१५२॥

152. Nothing is smaller than an atom; and nothing greater than the sky. Certainly one who says so, has not seen the supplicant, and the self-respecting.

याचितुर्गौरवं दातुर्मन्ये संक्रान्तमन्यथा ।
तदवस्थौ कथं स्यातामेतौ गुरुलघू तदा ॥१५३॥

153. I think that the self-respect of the supplicant goes over to the donor. Otherwise, how else could their positions have been high and low.

अधो जिघृक्षवो यान्ति यान्त्यूदूर्ध्वमाजिघृक्षवः ।
इति स्पष्टं वदन्तो वा नामोन्नामौ तुलान्तयोः ॥१५४॥

154. The supplicants (heavy with dependence upon others) sink low, and the non-supplicants, (light with independence) rise upwards. This is clearly proved by the going down and rising up of the scale-pans of a balance.

सस्वमाशासते सर्वे न स्वं तत्सर्वतर्पि यत् ।
अर्थिवैमुख्यसंपादि सस्वत्वान्निःस्वता वरम् ॥१५५॥

155. All men expect (something from) a man of wealth; there is no wealth which can satisfy all. Possession-less-ness is therefore superior to possession of wealth, which must disappoint (some) supplicant.

आशाखनिरतीवाभूदगाधा निधिभिश्च या ।
सापि येन समीभूता तत्ते मानधनं धनम् ॥१५६॥

156. That wealth of self-respect is thy wealth, which has made even (filled up) the cavity of desire, which could not be filled up even by the (nine) Nidhis, (treasures of a Chakravarti).

आशाखनिरगाधेयमधःकृतजगत्त्रया ।
उत्सर्प्योत्सर्प्य तत्रस्थानहो सद्भिः समीकृता ॥१५७॥

157. The ascetics have levelled up the pit of desires, which could not be filled up by the (objects of) the three worlds, by constantly removing (the desires) which found place there. This is wonderful.

विहितविधिना देहस्थित्यै तपांस्युपबृंहय-
न्नशनमपरैर्भक्त्या दत्तं क्वचित् कियदिच्छति ।
तदपि नितरां लज्जाहेतुः किलास्य महात्मनः
कथमयमहो गृह्णात्यन्यान्परिग्रहदुर्ग्रहान् ॥१५८॥

158. (An ascetic) while advancing his austerities, takes occasionally, in order to preserve the body, a little food given by others, out of religious devotion, in accordance with prescribed rules. Why! even that is very much a cause of shame to that high-souled (ascetic, for it makes him dependent on others). It is a great wonder then

how this (ascetic) accepts other worldly objects, fit to be discarded.

दातारो गृहचारिणः किल धनं देयं तदत्राशनं
गृह्णन्तः स्वशरीरतोऽपि विरताः सर्वोपकारेच्छया ।
लज्जैषैव मनस्विनां ननु पुनः कृत्वा कथं तत्फलं
रागद्वेषवशीभवन्ति तदिदं चक्रेश्वरत्वं कलेः ॥१५६॥

159. Here, the house-holders are donors and food is the only subject of gift. Those who accept it with the object of doing good to all have no attachment for even their own bodies. Even this (acceptance is) humiliation for the high-minded (sages). How then, (some of them) consider it (food) as the fruit of asceticism, and are moved by likes and dislikes? This is the supremacy of Kali age.

आमृष्टं सहजं तव त्रिजगतीबोधाधिपत्यं तथा
सौख्यं चात्मसमुद्भवं विनिहतं निर्मूलतः कर्मणा ।
दैन्यात्तद्विहितैस्त्वमिन्द्रियसुखैः सन्तृप्यसे निस्त्रपः
स त्वं यश्चिरयातनाकदशनैर्बद्धस्थितिस्तुष्यसि ॥१६०॥

160. Thy in-born power of knowing the three worlds has been eradicated, and the happiness arising from within thyself uprooted by Karma. If thou art pleased by maintaining (thy-self) with unsavoury food (acquired) after long sufferings, and gratified in (thy) meanness by sense-pleasures given by that Karma, thou art without shame, indeed.

तृष्णा भोगेषु चेद्भिक्षो सहस्वाल्पं स्वरेव ते ।
प्रतीक्ष्य पाकं किं पीत्वा पेया भुक्तिं विनाशये ॥१६१॥

161. Oh ascetic! If there be (in thee a) thirst for pleasures, have a little patience. Verily those (pleasures) will be thine in heaven. Why should one mar one's appetite by drinking water, without having waited for the serving up of (dishes)?

निर्धनत्वं धनं येषां मृत्युरेव हि जीवितम् ।
किं करोति विधिस्तेषां सतां ज्ञानैकचक्षुषाम् ॥१६२॥

162. What can Karma do to saints who see with discrimination, whose wealth is possession-less-ness and to whom death itself is life.

जीविताशा धनाशा च येषां तेषां विधिर्विधिः ।
किं करोति विधिस्तेषां येषामाशा निराशता ॥१६३॥

163. Karma is a ruler to those who desire life and aspire for wealth. What can Karma do to them, whose desire has been extinguished.

परां कोटिं समारूढौ द्वावेव स्तुतिनिन्दयोः ।
यस्त्यजेत्तपसे चक्रं यस्तपोविषयाशया ॥१६४॥

164. Only those two have reached the highest stages of praise and blame; one who renounces Empire for the sake of austerity, and the one who relinquishes austerity for sense-gratification.

त्यजतु तपसे चक्रं चक्री यतस्तपसः फलं
सुखमनुपमं स्वोत्थं (त्थं) नित्यं ततो न तदद्भुतम् ।
इदमिह महच्चित्रं यत्तद्विषं विषयात्मकं
पुनरपि सुधीस्त्यक्तं भोक्तुं जहाति महत्तपः ॥१६५॥

165. Since unrivalled eternal bliss, arising from one's ownself, is the fruit of austerities, an Emperor may renounce his kingdom for asceticism. There is no wonder in this. (But) this is a great wonder in this world that a wise man should relinquish noble austerity to feed again upon the poison of sense-pleasures, which had been renounced.

शय्यातलादपि तु कोऽपि भयं प्रपाता-
त्तुङ्गात्ततः खलु विलोक्य किलात्मपीड़ाम् ।
चित्रं त्रिलोकशिखरादपि दूरतुङ्गा-
द्धीमान्स्वयं न तपसः पतनाद्बिभेति ॥१६६॥

166. Fore-seeing injury to self, one is afraid of falling down even from a high bed-stead. It is a wonder

that the wise (ascetic) does not fear falling off from austerity, higher than the pinnacle of the three worlds.

विशुद्ध्यति दुराचारः सर्वोऽपि तपसा ध्रुवम् ।
करोति मलिनं तच्च किल सर्वाधरोऽपरः ॥१६७॥

**167.** Verily all sin is purified by austerities. But he is surely the vilest of all, who defiles that (austerity itself).

सन्त्येव कौतुकशतानि जगत्सु किन्तु
विस्मापकं तदलमेतदिह द्वयं नः ।
पीत्वामृतं यदि वमन्ति विसृष्टपुण्याः
संप्राप्य संयमनिधिं यदि च त्यजन्ति ॥१६८॥

**168.** There are hundreds of wonderful things in this world. To us these two are the most wonderful; the unfortunate men who vomit nectar after taking it, (and) those who reject the treasure of austerity, after having acquired it.

इह विनिहितबह्वारम्भबाह्योरुशत्रो-
रुपचितनिजशक्तेर्नापरः कोऽप्यपायः ।
अशनशयनयानस्थानदत्तावधानः
कुरु तव परिरक्षामान्तरान् हन्तुकामः ॥१६९॥

**169.** There is no other risk, here for one, who has subjugated the external powerful enemy of numerous occupations, and concentrated the soul force. Desirous of extirpating thy internal enemies, protect thyself from all sides, paying attention to food, sleep, movement, and posture.

अनेकान्तात्मार्थप्रसवफलभारातिविनते
वचः पर्णाकीर्णे विपुलनयशाखाशतयुते ।
समुत्तुङ्गे सम्यक् प्रततमतिमूले प्रतिदिनं
श्रुतस्कन्धे धीमान् रमयतु मनोमर्कटममुम् ॥१७०॥

**170.** A wise man should always beguile the mind-monkey on the very lofty scripture-tree, which is drooping down with the load of the fruit and flowers of substances dealt from many points of view, spreading with foliage of (sound) counsel, having hundreds of extensive branches of rules of Logic, and whose roots of sensitive knowledge have spread far and deep.

तदेव तदतद्रूपं प्राप्नुवन्न विरंस्यति ।
इति विश्वमनाद्यंतं चिन्तयेद्विश्ववित्सदा ॥१७१॥

**171.** One, (versed in all the Principles of Jainism should ever think that this universe is without a beginning and without an end. It is never destroyed; it remains the same (with reference to continuity of its substances) and not the same (having regard to modifications in the forms of substances).

एकमेकक्षणे सिद्धं ध्रौव्योत्पत्तिव्ययात्मकम् ।
अबाधितान्येतत्प्रत्ययान्यथानुपपत्तितः ॥१७२॥

**172.** It is an established truth that a substance is possessed of the three qualities of continuity (Dhrauvya) rise, (Utapada), and decay (Vyaya) at one and the same time, otherwise (we) cannot have the irrefutable belief that (a thing is) the same and a different one (at the same time).

न स्थास्नु न क्षणविनाशि न बोधमात्रं
नाभावमप्रतिहतप्रतिभासरोधात् ।
तत्त्वं प्रतिक्षणभवत्तदतत्स्वरूप-
माद्यन्तहीनमखिलं च तथा यथैकम् ॥१७३॥

**173.** Substance (in principle) is neither (altogether) permanent nor destructible, at every moment, nor knowable alone, nor (merely) non-existent, because (a one-sided view) is not irrefutably demonstrated. (Substance) is at every moment, the same and not the same, and without beginning and without end. (This is) as (true) with regard to all (substances) as (it is) with regard to one.

ज्ञानस्वभावः स्यादात्मा स्वभावावाप्तिरच्युतिः ।
तस्मादच्युतिमाकांक्षन् भावयेज्ज्ञानभावनाम् ॥१७४॥

**174.** The natural characteristic of the soul is knowledge. The possession of natural characteristic is without destruction. So one wishing indestructibility, should contemplate upon and attain (self) knowledge.

ज्ञानमेव फलं ज्ञाने ननु श्लाघ्यमनश्वरम् ।
अहो मोहस्य माहात्म्यमन्यदप्यत्र मृग्यते ॥१७५॥

**175.** Verily enlightenment (omniscience) is the adorable and indestructible fruit achievable by (right) knowledge. Great is the might of the deluding Karma, that even some other (fruit, such as sense-gratification, etc.) is here looked for.

शास्त्राग्नौ मणिवद्भव्यो विशुद्धो भाति निर्वृतः
अङ्गारवत् खलो दीप्तो मली वा भस्म वा भवेत् ॥१७६॥

**176.** A self-contented and pure person, fit to be liberated, glows (brightly) in the flame (light) of the scriptures, like a jewel. A wicked person, burning there like charcoal, turns either black or into ashes.

मुहुः प्रसार्य सज्ज्ञानं पश्यन् भावान् यथास्थितान् ।
प्रीत्यप्रीती निराकृत्य ध्यायेदध्यात्मविन्मुनिः ॥१७७॥

**177.** An ascetic, knowing the supreme nature of the soul, perceiving the essences (essential nature of things) as they are, extending his right knowledge again and again, and exterminating love and hate, should contemplate (upon the supreme self).

वेष्टनोद्वेष्टने यावत् तावद्भ्रान्तिर्भवार्णवे ।
आवृत्तिपरिवृत्ताभ्यां जन्तोर्मन्थानुकारिणः ॥१७८॥

**178.** The living being, like a churning stick, wanders in this ocean of births with goings and comings (births and rebirths) so long as there are the tying and untying (by the rope in case of the churning rod, and by Karmas in case of the living being).

मुच्यमानेन पाशेन भ्रान्तिर्बन्धश्च मन्थवत् ।
जन्तुस्तथासौ मोक्तव्यो येनाभ्रान्तिरबन्धनम् ॥१७९॥

179. The living being, like the churning stick, gets turning on (one side) and binding (on the other) when the rope is loosened. The rope is to be loosened in such a way that there be neither turning nor binding.

रागद्वेषकृताभ्यां जन्तोर्बन्धः प्रवृत्त्यवृत्तिभ्याम् ।
तत्त्वज्ञानकृताभ्यां ताभ्यामेवेक्ष्यते मोक्षः ॥१८०॥

180. The acquisitions and renunciations through attachment and hatred (cause) the binding of a living being. And these very (acquisitions and renunciations) lead to liberation, when accompanied with right-self-knowledge.

द्वेषानुरागबुद्धिर्गुणदोषकृता करोति खलु पापम् ।
तद्विपरीता पुण्यं तदुभयरहिता तयोर्मोक्षम् ॥१८१॥

181. The intellect disliking virtues and liking vices verily binds demerits; (and) merit, (when) acting contrary-wise. Free from both (like and dislike) (there is) liberation from both (the demeritorious and meritorious Karmas).

मोहबीजाद्रतिद्वेषौ बीजान् मूलाङ्कुराविव ।
तस्माज्ज्ञानाग्निना दाह्यं तदेतौ निर्दिधिक्षुणा ॥१८२॥

182. From the seed of delusion (spring) the two sprouts of attachment and hatred, just like roots and sprouts from a seed. So one desirous of extirpating these two, should burn down the (seed of delusion) by he fire of (self) knowledge.

पुराणो ग्रहदोषोत्थो गम्भीरः सगतिः सरुक् ।
त्यागजात्यादिना मोहव्रणः शुद्ध्यति रोहति ॥१८३॥

183. The deep, moving (the man in the four conditions of existence), painful and chronic boil of delusion, caused by the error of (attachment for) worldly objects, is cleared and healed up by such ointment as the renunciation (of non-self, realization of the self).

सुहृदः सुखयन्तः स्युर्दुःखयन्ता यदि द्विषः ।
सुहृदोऽपि कथं शोच्या द्विषो दुःखयितुं मृताः ॥१८४॥

**184**. If friends bring pleasures, and enemies bring miseries; then why should those enemies (wife, son, etc.,) be mourned, who died only to cause thee pain although they were (apparently) friends?

अपरमरणे मत्वात्मीयानलङ्घ्यतमे रुदन् ।
विलपतितरां स्वस्मिन् मृत्यौ तथास्य जडात्मनः॥
विभयमरणे भूयः साध्यं यशः परजन्म वा ।
कथमिति सुधीः शोकं कुर्यान्मृतेऽपि न केनचित् ॥१८५॥

**185.** This foolish man laments the inevitable death of others, thinking them as his own. And he laments still more on (thinking of) his own death. Renown and better life hereafter can be obtained by a fearless death. Why should a wise man grieve, on account of death even. None (should therefore grieve).

हानेः शोकस्ततो दुःखं लाभाद्रागस्ततः सुखम् ।
तेन हानावशोकः सन् सुखी स्यात् सर्वदा सुधीः ॥१८६॥

**186**. From loss (arises) sorrow, and there-from pain. From gain (arises) delight, and there-from pleasure. A wise man should therefore be always happy, not being touched by sorrow on account of loss.

सुखी सुखमिहान्यत्र दुःखी दुःखं समश्नुते ।
सुखं सकलसंन्यासो दुःखं तस्य विपर्ययः ॥१८७॥

**187**. In this and the next world, a happy man enjoys happiness, (and) an unhappy man experiences pain. Renunciation of all is happiness, and its contrary (is) misery.

मृत्योर्मृत्यवन्तरप्राप्तिरुत्पत्तिरिह देहिनाम् ।
तत्र प्रमुदितान्मन्ये पाश्चात्ये पक्षपातिनः ॥१८८॥

**188**. In this world birth after death is the origin of another death, because death is the very necessary cause of birth and *vice versa*. I think that those, who rejoice on birth are partial to the other (*viz*, death).

अधीत्य सकलं श्रुतं चिरमुपास्य घोरं तपो
यदीच्छसि फलं तयोरिह हि लाभपूजादिकम् ।
छिनत्सि सुतपस्तरोः प्रसवमेव शून्याशयः
कथं समुपलप्स्यसे सुरसमस्य पक्वं फलम् ॥१८९॥

**189.** Having studied all the scriptures and having undergone severe austerities, if thou as their fruit, wishest wealth, respect, etc., in this very world, then, O devoid of discrimination, thou takest away the very flower of the beautiful tree of austerity. How canst thou have its juicy ripe fruit?

तथा श्रुतमधीष्व शश्वदिह लोकपंक्तिं विना
शरीरमपि शोषय प्रथितकायसंक्लेशनैः ।
कषायविषयद्विषो विजयसे यथा दुर्जयान्
शमं हि फलमामनन्ति मुनयस्तपःशास्त्रयोः ॥१९०॥

**190.** Always study the scriptures without (caring for the common) line of the people (wordly fame and respect), and mortify the body by severe austerities, in such a way, that thou mayst subjugate thy invincible enemies, the sense-enjoyments. The sages regard only passionless-ness as the fruit of austerities and study of scriptures.

दृष्ट्वा जनं व्रजसि किं विषयाभिलाषं
स्वल्पोऽप्यसौ तव महज्जनयत्यनर्थम् ।
स्नेहाद्युपक्रमजुषो हि यथातुरस्य
दोषो निषिद्धचरणं न तथेतरस्य ॥१९१॥

**191.** Following (common) people why dost thou crave for sense enjoyments? Even a little of that (craving) does thee great harm. The taking in of oily things prohibited for the sick under medical treatment, is injurious (to him); not so to others.

अहितविहितप्रीतिः प्रीतं कलत्रमपि स्वयं
सकृदपकृतं श्रुत्वा सद्यो जहाति जनोऽप्ययम् ।

स्वहितनिरतः साक्षाद्दोषं समीक्ष्य भवे भवे
विषयविषवद्ग्रासाभ्यासं कथं कुरुते बुधः ॥१९२॥

**192.** Even this (ordinary) man who is greatly swayed by affection, immediately gives up himself, even his beloved wife, on hearing of (her) misconduct. How does this wise man engaged in self-advancement, take the poisoned food of sense-pleasures having clearly realised their injurious nature in various births?

आत्मन्नात्मविलोपनात्मचरितैरासीद्दुरात्मा चिरं
स्वात्मास्याःसकलात्मनीनचरितैरात्मीकृतैरात्मनः ।
आत्मेत्यां परमात्मतां प्रतिपतन्प्रत्यात्मविद्यात्मकः
स्वात्मोत्थात्मसुखो निषीदसि लसन्नध्यात्ममध्यात्मना १९३

**193.** O soul, thou hast long been vicious, by self injurious self-actions. Be thy own self, by adopting all the self-inherent qualities of the soul. Having obtained thy own supreme soul-hood, and identified with all self-knowledge, and realizing soul-happiness, arising from thy own self, thou, resplendent with the inner self, shalt stay in thy own self.

अनेन सुचिरं पुरा त्वमिह दासवद्वाहित-
स्ततोऽनशनसामिभुक्तरसवर्जनादिक्रमैः ।
क्रमेण विलयावधिस्थिरतपोविशेषैरिदं
कदर्थय शरीरकरिपुमिवाद्य हस्तागतम् ॥१९४॥

**194.** Before now, thou hast long been driven like a slave by this body. So by fasting, scanty meals, renunciation of Rasas (salt, butter, sugar, etc.,) and the other forms of austerities, mortify this body gradually (preserving it till death), as if it were an enemy, now fallen in thy hands.

आदौ तनोर्जननमत्र हतेन्द्रियाणि
काङ्क्षन्ति तानि विषयान् विषमाश्च मानः ।
हानिप्रयासभयपापकुयोनिदाः स्यु-
र्मूलं ततस्तनुरनर्थपरम्पराणाम् ॥ १९५ ॥

195. At first the body is formed. The wretched senses then desire (their respective) gratifications. Sense-enjoyments cause loss of self-respect, misery, fear, demerit, and undesirable birth places. Thus the body is unfortunately, the root of a series of evils.

शरीरमपि पुष्णन्ति सेवन्ते विषयानपि ।
नास्त्यहो दुष्करं नृणां विषाद्वाञ्छन्ति जीवितम् ॥ १९६ ॥

196. They nourish such a body (and) resort to such sense-pleasures. Oh there is nothing which men would not do. They wish to live by taking poison.

इतस्ततश्च त्रस्यन्तो विभावर्यां यथा मृगाः ।
वनाद्विशन्त्युपग्रामं कलौ कष्टं तपस्विनः ॥ १९७ ॥

197. It is a great pity, that in this Kali age, ascetics, having roamed here and there, in the forest, like deer, enter at night,the suburbs of a habitation (for safety).

वरं गार्हस्थ्यमेवाद्य तपसो भाविजन्मनः ।
सुस्त्रीकटाक्षलुण्टाकैर्लुप्तवैराग्यसंपदः ॥ १९८ ॥

198. Here, the householder's life is better than (such) asceticism, (as is) the cause of future births, and is robbed of its wealth of non-attachment by robbers (in the form of) beautiful women's side-long glances.

स्वार्थभ्रंशं त्वमविगणयंस्त्यक्तलज्जाभिमानः
संप्राप्तोऽस्मिन् परिभवशतैर्दुःखमेतत्कलत्रम् ।
नान्वेति त्वां पदमपि पदाद्विप्रलुब्धोऽसि भूयः
सख्यं साधो यदि हि मतिमान्माग्रहीर्विग्रहेण ॥ १९९ ॥

199. Thou hast been repeatedly deprived of thy position by this body, (for which) thou, bereft of shame and self-respect, not minding loss of self-advancement, and after hundreds of humiliations, hast taken this evil-bringing woman. O sage, if thou art wise, do not befriend (the body) which does not follow thee even a step (after death.)

न कोऽप्यन्योऽन्येन व्रजति समवायं गुणवता
गुणी केनापि त्वं समुपगतवान् रूपिभिरमी ।
न ते रूपं ते यानुपव्रजसि तेषां गतमति-
स्ततश्छेद्यो भेद्यो भवसि भवदुःखे भववने ॥ २०० ॥

200. Any one substance (guṉi, dravya) does not merge in any other substance (guṉa-wata). Thou hast merged in these material substances (having form). Their nature is not thine. Oh fool, thou followest them, and therefore art cut and pierced in this worldly forest of manifold miseries.

माता जातिः पिता मृत्युराधिव्याधी सहोद्गतौ ।
प्रान्ते जन्तोर्जरा मित्रं तथाप्याशा शरीरके ॥ २०१ ॥

201. Birth is, the mother; death, father; mental and physical sufferings, brothers ; and decrepitude is the friend of this living being in the last stage. And yet there is love for the body.

शुद्धोऽप्यशेषविषयावगमोऽप्यमूर्तोऽ-
प्यात्मन् त्वमप्यतितरामशुचीकृतोऽसि ।
मूर्त्तं सदा शुचि विचेतनमन्यदत्र
किं वा न दूषयति धिग्धिगिदं शरीरम् ॥ २०२ ॥

202. O soul, even thou, being, (by nature, pure, cognisant of all things, and immaterial, art greatly polluted (by the body). What other thing in this world, does this ever-impure, lifeless, and material (body) not vitiate? Fie on such a body!

हा हतोऽसितरां जन्तो येनास्मिंस्तव सांप्रतम् ।
ज्ञानं कायाशुचिज्ञानं तत्त्यागः किल साहसम् ॥ २०३ ॥

203. (True) knowledge is to know this body to be impure. Its renunciation is real valour. O living being, thou hast now been greatly deceived here, by this (body).

अपि रोगादिभिर्वृद्धैर्न मुनिः खेदमृच्छति ।
उडुपस्थस्य कः क्षोभः प्रवृद्धेऽपि नदीजले ॥ २०४ ॥

204. An ascetic is not distressed even by increase in diseases. What fear is there to one, sitting in a boat, even if the water of the river be high?

जातामयः प्रतिविधाय तनौ वसेद्वा
नो चेत्तनुं त्यजतु वा द्वितयी गतिः स्यात् ।
लग्नाग्निमावसति वह्निमपोह्य गेहं
निर्हाय वा व्रजति तत्र सुधीः किमास्ते ॥ २०५ ॥

205. A sick man should take medicines and live in the body. Otherwise he should renounce the body (by a pious-death, which) is the (other) alternative. A wise man should continue living in a house, which has caught fire after putting out that fire, or abandoning it should go away (elsewhere). Why should he live there?

शिरस्थं भारमुत्तार्य्य स्कन्धे कृत्वा सुयत्नतः ।
शरीरस्थेन भारेण अज्ञानी मन्यते सुखम् ॥ २०६ ॥

206. An ignorant man, taking up the load from the head with great difficulty, and placing it on the shoulder, thinks himself happy, (though) the load is still on the body.

यावदस्ति प्रतीकारस्तावत्कुर्यात् प्रतिक्रियाम् ।
तथाप्यनुपशान्तानामनुद्वेगः प्रतिक्रिया ॥ २०७ ॥

207. A remedy should be sought, so long as a thing is remediable. And for those who are incurable, the (only) remedy is to be indifferent.

यदा यदा भवेज्जन्मी त्यक्त्वा मुक्तो भविष्यति ।
शरीरमेव तत्त्याज्यं किं शेषैः क्षुद्रकल्पनैः ॥ २०८ ॥

203. One would attain liberation after getting rid of the bodies, (Taijasa, and Kármaṉa), in company with which he is subject to births. They must be got rid of. What use is there in other petty conjectures.

नयत्सर्वाशुचिप्रायं शरीरमपि पूज्यताम् ।
सोऽप्यात्मा येन न स्पृश्यो दुश्चरित्रं धिगस्तु तत् ॥ २०९ ॥

**209.** The soul makes even that body, which is all-impurity, an object of worship. Fie on that wicked (body), by which even such a soul is made untouchable.

रसादिराद्यो भागः स्यात् ज्ञानावृत्यादिरन्वितः ।
ज्ञानादयस्तृतीयस्तु संसार्य्येवं त्रयात्मकः ॥ २१० ॥

**210.** A mundane soul has three parts, thus :—the first is fluid, and (blood, bone, etc.); the other is the knowledge-obscuring, etc., (Karma); the third is knowledge, etc., (innate qualities of the soul).

भागत्रयमिदं नित्यमात्मानं बन्धवर्त्तिनम् ।
भागद्वयात् पृथक्कर्त्तुं यो जानाति स तत्त्ववित् ॥ २११ ॥

**211.** He is the knower of the principles (7 Tattvas), who knows how to separate the eternal soul, existing in bondage, and having three parts, from the (first) two parts (above-stated).

करोतु न चिरं घोरं तपः क्लेशासहो भवान् ।
चित्तसाध्यान् कषायारीन्न जयेद्यत्तदज्ञता ॥ २१२ ॥

**212.** (If) you cannot bear hardships, do not practise long, rigorous austerities. It is thy ignorance that thou dost not conquer the enemies, passions, which can be subjugated by (control of) mind.

हृदयसरसि यावन्निर्मलेऽप्यत्यगाधे
वसति खलु कषायग्राहचक्रं समन्तात् ।
श्रयति गुणगणोऽयं तन्न तावद्विशङ्कं
समदमयमशेषैस्तान् विजेतुं यतस्व ॥ २१३ ॥

**213.** So long as the clear and unfathomable lake of the heart is throughout infested with the host of crocodiles of passions, the host of (pure) attributes cannot fearlessly resort to it. Strive to subjugate them (the passions) with equanimity, self-control, renunciation, and the like.

हित्वा हेतुफले किलात्र सुधियस्तां सिद्धिमामुत्रिकीं
वाञ्छन्तः स्वयमेव साधनतया शंसन्ति शान्तं मनः।
तेषामाखुबिडालिकेति तदिदं धिग्धिक्कलेःप्राभवं
येनैतेऽपि फलद्वयप्रलयनाद्दूरं विपर्य्यासिताः ॥ २१४ ॥

214. (There are) here such clever men, who desire to attain perfection hereafter, but having missed the true cause and effect, boast of having themselves acquired a peaceful mind. This (conduct) of theirs is like that of the cat and the mice. Fie, on the supremacy of Kaliyuga, by which these men have been greatly deceived, and deprived of the (true) fruit of both (the worlds).

उद्युक्तस्त्वं तपस्यस्यधिकमभिभवंस्त्वामगच्छन्कषायाः
प्राभूद्बोधोऽप्यगाधो जलमिव जलधौ किन्तु दुर्लक्ष्यमन्यैः।
निर्व्यूढेऽपि प्रवाहे सलिलमिव मनाग्निम्नदेशेष्ववश्यं
मात्सर्य्यन्ते स्वतुल्यैर्भवति परवशाद्दुर्जयं तज्जहीहि ॥ २१५ ॥

215. Thou art prepared for austerities; the passions have been greatly humiliated by thee, thou hast acquired knowledge, deep like waters of the ocean, but must give up jealousy for thy equal, which is due to other causes (Karmas), and is difficult to subdue, and cannot be noticed by others, like water in very low and invisible flow of (the ocean).

चित्तस्थमप्यनवबुध्य हरेण जाड्या
त्क्रुद्ध्वा बहिः किमपि दग्धमनङ्गबुद्ध्या।
घोरामवाप स हि तेन कृतामवस्थां
क्रोधोदयाद्भवति कस्य न कार्य्यहानिः ॥ २१६ ॥

216. Shiva, not knowing that cupid lived in the heart burnt, out of anger, something external mistaking it for the God of Love. He had to experience excruciating pain caused by that cupid. Whose object is not lost by (operation of) anger.

चक्रं विहाय निजदक्षिणबाहुसंस्थं
यत्प्राव्रजन्ननु तदैव स तेन मुक्तः ।
क्लेशं तमाप किल बाहुबली चिराय
मानो मनागपि हतिं महतीं करोति ॥ २१७ ॥

217. Leaving the boomerang (Chakra) which had alighted on his right arm, Bahubali became an ascetic, and then only did he attain Liberation. Even he suffered long (before attaining omniscience, as he had a tinge of pride in him). Even slight pride does great harm

**Commentary.**

Bahu-bali was the younger son of Rishabha Deva, the first Tírthankara, while Bharata was the eldest. Bharata having been worsted in a trial of strength with him , hurled at him the Chakra, which instead of harming him, alighted on his right arm. Bahu-bali was however sorry for having dishonoured his elder brother Bharata, and considering all worldly ambition as frivolous, he renounced all temporal possessions, and adopted asceticism, to obtain omniscience. He continued to observe meditation for one whole year, at a stretch, but did not obtain omniscience, because there was left in him a tinge of pride that although he had relinquished all, he was still standing on the ground owned by Bharata. When Bharata having been told of this, at the Samavasarnam of Shri Rishabha Deva, went and bowed to him, and told him that earth belonged to nobody, the pride was gone, and Bahu-bali immediately attained omniscience.

सत्यं वाचि मतौ श्रुतं हृदि दया शौर्य्यं भुजे विक्रमो
लक्ष्मीर्दानमनूनमर्थिनिचये मार्गो गतिर्निर्वृते ।
येषां प्रागजनीह तेऽपि निरहङ्काराः श्रुतेर्गोचरा-
श्चित्रं संप्रति लेशतोऽपि न गुणास्तेषां तथाप्युद्धताः ॥ २१८ ॥

218. Formerly, on this earth were born persons, who had truth in (their) word, knowledge of the scriptures in their intellect, compassion in their heart, bravery and fortitude in the arm, wealth for large charity to needy persons, and who trod in the path free from worldly attachments. Even such (great persons) have been described in the scriptures to have been free from pride. It is a great

wonder, that now-a-days those who do not possess even slight virtues, (are found) to be over-bearing.

वसति भुवि समस्तं सापि संधारितान्यै-
रुदरमुपनिविष्टा सा च ते चापरस्य ।
तदपि किल परेषां ज्ञानकोणे निलीनं
वहति कथमिहान्यो गर्वमात्माधिकेषु ॥ २१९ ॥

219 Everything dwells on this earth. That (earth) too is supported by others (*i.e.*, the three atmospheres). And that (earth) and those (atmospheres) are in the maw of another (*i.e.*, space). That (space) too is in a corner of the knowledge of others (*i.e.*, the all-knowing). How (then) can a man entertain pride, (when there are) greater ones than himself in this world?

यशोमारीचीयं कनकमृगमायामलिनितं
हतोऽश्वत्थामोक्त्या प्रणयिलघुरासीद्यमसुतः ।
सकृष्णः कृष्णोऽभूत्कपटबटुवेषेणनितरा-
मपिच्छद्माल्पं तद्विषमिव हि दुग्धस्य महतः ॥ २२० ॥

220. The fame of Marichi, was sullied or stained by his deceit in assuming the garb of a golden deer. Yudhishthira was lowered in the estimation of his friends for saying (deceitfully) "Ashvatthâma is killed"; and Krishna's reputation was tarnished by (his) deceitfully adopting the form of a little boy. So even a particle of deceit (injures) high qualities, just like a (little) poison in (a quantity of) milk.

भेयं मायामहागर्तान्मिथ्याघनतमोमयात् ।
यस्मिन् लीना न लक्ष्यन्ते क्रोधादिविषमाहयः ॥ २२१ ॥

221. One should be apprehensive of the deep pit of deceit enveloped in the pitchy darkness of falsehood. The horrible cobras of anger, etc. (the Passions) living in its depth are not visible.

प्रच्छन्नकर्म मम कोऽपि न वेत्ति धीमान्
ध्वंसं गुणस्य महतोऽपि हि मेति मंस्थाः ।
कामं गिलन् धवलदीधितिधौतदाहो
गूढोऽप्यबोधि न विधुः सविधुन्तुदः कैः ॥ २२२ ॥

222. Do not think "no clever person even knows my secret sins", and "how will this mar my high qualities." Who does not know that the invisible Rahu swallows wholly the white-rayed and soothing moon.

वनचरभयाद्धावन् दैवाल्लताकुलबालधिः
किल जडतया लोलो वालव्रजे विचलं स्थितः ।
बत स चमरस्तेन प्राणैरपि प्रवियोजितः
परिणततृषां प्रायेणैवंविधा हि विपत्तयः ॥ २२३ ॥

223. A Chámara deer, while running away in fear of a Bheela, had her hairy tail entangled in creepers. Being foolishly fond of the hair-tuft, she stood motionless. Alas! for that (attachment to the hair) she was deprived even of her life. Generally such are the calamities of those, who are afflicted with greed.

विषयविरतिः संगत्यागः कषायविनिग्रहः
शमयमदमास्तत्त्वाभ्यासस्तपश्चरणोद्यमः ।
नियमितमनोवृत्तिर्भक्तिर्जिनेषु दयालुता
भवति कृतिनः संसाराब्धेस्तटे निकटे सति ॥ २२४ ॥

224. When the shore of the ocean of the cycle of existence is close by, the fortunate man has aversion to sense-gratifications, renounces all possessions, subjugates the passions, has tranquility, vows, self-control, practice of self-contemplation, pursuit of austerities, duly ordained mental activity, devotion to the conquerors, and compassion.

यमनियमनितान्तः शान्तबाह्यान्तरात्मा
परिणमितसमाधिः सर्वसत्त्वानुकम्पी ।

विहितहितामिताशी क्लेशजालं समूलं
दहति निहतनिद्रो निश्चिताध्यात्मसारः ॥ २२५ ॥

225. One who is engaged in vows, temporary, and life-long, has acquired internal and external peace, has practised equanimity, has compassion for all the living beings; takes limited and helpful meals, has annihilated sleep, and has ascertained the essence of the nature of the soul, and burns the host of miseries to the very root.

समधिगतसमस्ताः सर्वसावद्यदूराः
स्वहितनिहितचित्ताः शान्तसर्वप्रचाराः ।
स्वपरसफलजल्पाः सर्वसंकल्पमुक्ताः
कथमिह न विमुक्तेर्भाजनं ते विमुक्ताः ॥ २२६ ॥

226. Why should not such unattached (recluses) here, deserve liberation, who are proficient in all the principles and who abstain from all sins, who are absorbed in self-advancement, who have controlled all their senses, who are free from all sorts of illusions, and whose speech is beneficial to self and others.

दासत्वं विषयप्रभोर्गतवतामात्मापि येषां पर-
स्तेषां भो गुणदोषशून्यमनसां किं तत्पुनर्नश्यति ।
भेतव्यं भवतैव यस्य भुवनप्रद्योति रत्नत्रयं
भ्राम्यन्तीन्द्रियतस्कराश्च परितस्त्वं तन्मुहुर्जागृहि ॥ २२७ ॥

227. What more can those indiscriminate persons have to lose who have become slaves to the lord of the sense-pleasures, and whose soul itself has become perverse? But thou who hast got the world-illuminating three gems, (right-belief, knowedge, and conduct) should fear the surrounding robbers (in the garb of) sense-desires. So, thou shouldst always be awake.

रम्येषु वस्तुवनितादिषु वीतमोहो
मुह्येद् वृथा किमिति संयमसाधनेषु ।

धीमान् किमामयभयात्परिहृत्य भुक्तिं
पीत्वौषधं व्रजति जातुचिदप्यजीर्णम् ॥ २२८ ॥

228. Why shouldst thou, (who art) beyond attachment to beautiful women, and other objects, have futile attachment for the instruments of austerity (the alms-bowl, broom of peacock-feathers, etc)? Does ever a prudent man, who takes no food for fear of disease, get indigestion by taking (too much) of medicine.

तपः श्रुतमिति द्वयं बहिरुदीर्य रूढं यथा
कृषीफलमिवालये समुपनीयते स्वात्मनि ।
कृषीवल इवोत्थितं करणचोरव्याधादिभि-
स्तदा हि मनुते यतिः स्वकृतकृत्यतां धीरधीः ॥ २२९ ॥

229. A wise ascetic considers his exertions successful only, when he has withdrawn from outside both his advanced austerity and knowledge, and well-placed them in self absorption, above the attacks of thieves and robbers, (in the form of) the senses, like a farmer, who has safely brought home the harvest.

दृष्टार्थस्य न मे किमप्ययमिति ज्ञानावलेपादमुं
नोपेक्षस्व जगत्त्रयैकडमरं निःशेषयाशाद्विषम् ।
पश्याम्भोनिधिमप्यगाधसलिलं चावाध्यते वाडवः
क्रोडीभूतविपक्षकस्य जगति प्रायेण शान्तिः कुतः ॥ २३० ॥

230. In the pride of knowledge that this desire-enemy (can do) nothing to me, who am versed in scriptures, thou shouldst not be indifferent to it, but shouldst extirpate that one scourge for the three worlds. Lo! the submarine fire troubles even the unfathomable water of the ocean. How can one, lying in the lap of the enemy, possibly have calmness, in the world?

स्नेहानुबद्धहृदया ज्ञानचरित्रान्वितोऽपि न श्लाघ्यः ।
दीप इवापादयिता कज्जलमलिनस्य कार्य्यस्य ॥ २३१ ॥

231. A person with a heart bound in attachment, though possessed of knowledge and conduct, is not worthy of praise, like the lamp, whose dark action is the production of soot.

रतेररतिमायातः पुनररतिमुपागतः ।
तृतीयं पदमप्राप्य बालिशो बत सीदसि ॥ २३२ ॥
तावद्दुःखाग्नितप्तात्माऽयःपिण्ड इव सीदसि ।
निर्वासिनिर्वृताम्भोधौ यावत्त्वं न निमज्जसि ॥ २३३ ॥

232-233. (Many times) didst thou become repulsed from attachment, and again became attached. It is a great pity that thou, a fool, not having acquired the third stage, (*i.e.*), freedom from attachment and repulsion, art in distress. Thou, like a ball of iron, art pained, being consumed by the fire of attachment, so long as thou art not immersed, in the ocean of the happiness of liberation.

मंक्षु मोक्षं सुसम्यक्त्वं सत्यंकारस्वसात्कृतम् ।
ज्ञानचारित्रसाकल्यमूलेन स्वकरे कुरु ॥ २३४ ॥

234. Promptly take liberation in thy hand, which can be had by (paying) the earnest money of Right-belief and the price of perfect knowledge and conduct.

अशेषमद्वैतमभोग्यभोग्यं निवृत्तिवृत्योः परमार्थकोट्याम् ।
अभोग्यभोग्यात्मविकल्पबुद्ध्या निवृत्तिमभ्यस्यतु मोक्षकांक्षी ॥

235. The whole of this one (world) is unenjoyable having regard to (the principle of) renunciation, and is enjoyable with regard to attachment (to it). One desirous of liberation should practise renunciation of the highest order, having himself known the alternative nature of its enjoyability and unenjoyability.

निवृत्तिं भावयेद्यावन्निवर्त्यं तदभावतः ।
न वृत्तिर्न निवृत्तिश्च तदेवपदमव्ययम् ॥ २३६ ॥

236. One should cherish renunciation so long as total non-attachment is not acquired. (When) there is

neither attachment nor renunciation, it is the indestructable stage, *i. e*, (liberation).

रागद्वेषौ प्रवृत्तिः स्यान्निवृत्तिस्तन्निषेधनम् ।
तौ च बाह्यार्थसम्बद्धौ तस्मात्तांश्च परित्यजेत् ॥ २३७ ॥

237. Love and hate constitute attachment; doing away with them is Renunciation. They both are associated with external objects, and so they should also be discarded.

भावयामि भवाऽऽवर्त्ते भावनाः प्रागभाविताः ।
भावये भाविता नेति भवाभावाय भावनाः ॥ २३८ ॥

238. In this whirl of transmigrations, for destruction of mundane existences, I cherish thoughts (of right-belief, etc.,) never cherished before, and do not cherish those thoughts (of wrong-belief, etc.,) hitherto cherished.

शुभाशुभे पुण्यपापे सुखदुःखे च षट्त्रयम् ।
हितमाद्यमनुष्ठेयं शेषत्रयमथाहितम् ॥ २३९ ॥

239. Good and bad (actions), merit and demerit (Karmas), and pleasure and pain (their fruits), are six. The first (of each) of the three (pairs) is beneficial and worth following; and the remaining three are injurious.

तत्राप्याद्यं परित्याज्यं शेषौ न स्तः स्वतः स्वयम् ।
शुभं च शुद्धे त्यक्त्वान्ते प्राप्नोति परमं पदम् ॥ २४० ॥

240. Then, again, the first (good activity) also is to be given up. The remaining (two sets) cease to exist by themselves. By giving up the good (activity), and attaining the summit of purity, one gets the supreme status (liberation).

अस्त्यात्मास्तमितादिबन्धनगतस्तद्बन्धनान्यास्रवै-
स्ते क्रोधादिकृताः प्रमादजनिताः क्रोदादयस्तेऽव्रतात् ।
मिथ्यात्वोपचितात् स एव समलः कालादिलब्धौ क्वचित्
सम्यक्त्वव्रतदक्षताकलुषतायोगैः क्रमान्मुच्यते ॥ २४१ ॥

**241.** Soul does exist, (and) it is under bondage (of Karmas) from (time) which has no beginning. That bondage is from the inflow (of Karmic matter), (the inflow) is caused by anger and other (passions); anger, etc., arise from carelessness. This (carelessness) is due to vowlessness; that (vowlessness) (exists under) influence of wrong-belief, such impure (soul), sometimes, on getting (proper) occasion, etc., is gradually liberated by the combination of right-belief, the excellence of vows, and passionlessness.

ममेदमहमस्येति प्रीतिरीतिरिवोत्थिता ।
क्षेत्रे क्षेत्रीयते यावत्तावत्का सा तपःफले ॥ २४२ ॥

**242.** The affection that this (body) is mine, and I am its, arises like a great calamity. What hope is there, for the fruition of austerities so long as (the soul) considers (himself) identified with the body.

मामन्यमन्यं मां मत्वा भ्रान्तो भ्रान्तौ भवार्णवे ।
नान्योऽहमहमेवाहमन्योऽन्योऽन्योऽहमस्ति न ॥ २४३ ॥

**243.** Believing, under delusion, that "I am another," "Another is me," I wander in the ocean of births. "I am not another," "I am I;" "another is another," "another is not me."

बन्धो जन्मनि येन येन निबिडं निष्पादितो वस्तुना
बाह्यार्थैकरतेः पुरापरिणतप्रज्ञात्मनः साम्प्रतम् ।
तत्तत्तन्निधनाय साधनमभूद्वैराग्यकाष्ठास्पृशो
दुर्बोधं हि तदन्यदेव विदुषामप्राकृतं कौशलम् ॥ २४४ ॥

**244.** Through whatever objects, in this world, bondage was tightened, heretofore in one, who was attached to external things, he has now obtained true knowledge; and those very (objects) have, on attainment of the fullest non-attachment, become instruments for destruction of that (bondage). Verily wrong-knowledge, and uncommon excellence of the learned, are different (things).

अधिकः क्वचिदाश्लेषः क्वचिद्धीनः क्वचित्समः ।
क्वचिद्विश्लेष एवायं बन्धमोक्षक्रमो मतः ॥ २४५ ॥

245. Combination (of Karmas is varying in quantity), sometimes increasing, sometimes decreasing, sometimes becoming equal, and sometimes there is separation only. Thus should be known the succession of bondage and liberation. (For details see Tattvártha Sútra, and Gommatasára).

यस्य पुण्यं च पापं च निष्फलं गलति स्वयम् ।
स योगी तस्य निर्वाणं न तस्य पुनरास्रवः ॥ २४६ ॥

246. He, whose merit and demerit (Karmas) exhaust themselves without bearing fruit is a (true) ascetic. He will never have the Karmic inflow, and will attain liberation.

महातपस्तडागस्य संभृतस्य गुणाम्भसा ।
मर्य्यादापालिबन्धेऽल्पामप्युपेक्षिष्ट मास्त्रतिम् ॥ २४७ ॥

247. Do not allow even a slight breach in the right conduct, (which is) the embankment of the great reservoir of austerity, filled with the waters of attributes (right-belief, etc).

दृढगुप्तिकपाटसंवृतिर्धृतिभित्तिर्मतिपादसंभृतिः ।
यतिरल्पमपि प्रपद्य रन्ध्रं कुटिलैर्विक्रियते गृहाकृतिः ॥ २४८ ॥

248. An ascetic is like a house, protected by the doors of strict restraint (of body, mind and speech), having the walls of fortitude, and the foundation of knowledge. He is attacked by wicked (passions), (if they) get even a small hole (defect) in his (conduct).

स्वान्दोषान्हन्तुमुद्युक्तस्तपोभिरतिदुर्द्धरैः ।
तानेव पोषयत्यज्ञः परदोषकथाशनैः ॥ २४९ ॥

249. Though determined to remove his faults by austere penance, the fool nourishes those very faults by the food of scandalizing others.

दोषः सर्वगुणाकरस्य महतो दैवानुरोधात्क्वचि-
ज्जातो यद्यपि चन्द्रलाञ्छनसमस्तं द्रष्टुमन्धोऽप्यलम् ।
द्रष्टाप्नोति न तावदस्य पदवीमिन्दोः कलङ्कं जग-
द्विश्वं पश्यति तत्प्रभाप्रकटितं किं कोऽप्यगात्तत्पदम् ॥ २५० ॥

250. When an ascetic, a great repository of all qualifications may by chance have a defect, under influence of past Karma, although the defect is like the spot in the moon, even a blind (*i.e.*, indiscriminate) man notices that. The on-looker need not reach his (the ascetic's position to notice the defect.) The whole world sees the spot in the moon, made prominent by her light. Did any one go to her place (in the moon, to see the spot)?

यद्यदाचरितं पूर्वं तत्तदज्ञानचेष्टितम् ।
उत्तरोत्तरविज्ञानाद्योगिनः प्रतिभासते ॥ २५१ ॥

251. Through gradually growing knowledge, all that is done in the past appears to an ascetic to be the action of ignorance.

अपि सुतपसामाशावल्लीशिखा तरुणायते
भवति हि मनोमूले यावन्ममत्वजलार्द्रता ।
इति कृतधियः कृच्छ्रारम्भैश्चरन्ति निरन्तरं
चिरपरिचिते देहेऽप्यस्मिन्नतीव गतस्पृहाः ॥ २५२ ॥

252. So long as there is moisture of attachment, at the root (of the tree) of mind, the tip of the creeper of Desire, keeps fresh even in great ascetics. Knowing this, those, who are quite unattached, always deal strictly even with the long long familiar body.

क्षीरनीरवदभेदरूपतस्तिष्ठतोरपि च देहदेहिनोः ।
भेद एव यदि भेदवत्स्वलं बाह्यवस्तुषु वदात्र का कथा ॥ २५३ ॥

253. When (by engaging in deep meditation), there is a difference between the body and the embodied (soul itself), even though they are inseparably connected like

milk and water, then what would you say of the marked differences which these other external things possess.

तप्तोऽहं देहसंयोगाज्जलं वानलसंगमात् ।
इह देहं परित्यज्य शीतीभूताः शिवैषिणः ॥ २५४ ॥

254. I am heated by the connection of this body, like water in association with fire. Those who long for happiness became cool here by leaving (attachment with) this body.

अनादिचयसंवृद्धो महामोहो हृदि स्थितः ।
सम्यग्योगेन यैर्वान्तस्तेषामूर्ध्वं विशुद्ध्यति ॥ २५५ ॥

255. Purified is the end of those who by proper meditative application have cast out the great delusion sealed in the heart and grown up by accumulations (of Karmas) from eternal time.

एकैश्वर्यमिहैकतामभिमतावाप्तिं शरीरच्युतिं
दुःखं दुष्कृतनिष्कृतिं सुखमलं संसारसौख्यासनम् ।
सर्वत्यागमहोत्सवव्यतिकरं प्राणव्ययं पश्यताम्
किं तद्यन्नसुखाय तेन सुखिनः सत्यं सदा साधवः ॥ २५६ ॥

256. What thing in this world is there, which is not conducive to the well-being of such (ascetics), as regard identification (with the self) as the only sovereignty, the destruction of the body as the attainment of the desired object, the evil from bad deeds as painful, the renunciation of wordly enjoyments as happiness; abandonment of everything as great joy, and attachment as death. Truly, the ascetics are always happy.

आकृष्योग्रतपोबलैरुदयगो (गं) पुच्छं यदानीयतं
तत्कर्म स्वयमागतं यदि विदः को नाम खेदस्ततः ।
यातव्यो विजिगीषुणा यदि भवेदारम्भकोऽरिः स्वयं
वृद्धिः प्रत्युत नेतुरप्रतिहता तद्विग्रहे कः क्षयः ॥ २५७ ॥

257. If that Karma which is destroyed by bringing it to (premature) fruition by severe austerities, has itself

arrived at its maturity, then what grief should a wise man feel for that? One desirous of vanquishing his foe should himself meet him. If that (foe) advances himself, what loss can there be in a conflict for him, who is himself advancing unchecked.

एकाकित्वप्रतिज्ञाः सकलमपि समुत्सृज्य सर्व सहत्वात्
भ्रान्त्याचिन्त्याः सहायं तनुमिव सहसालोच्य किंचित्सलज्जाः।
सज्जीभूताः स्वकार्य्यें तदपगमविधिं बद्धपल्यङ्कबन्धाः
ध्यायन्ति ध्वस्तमोहा गिरिगहनगुहा गुह्यगेहे नृसिंहाः ॥२५८॥

258. Those who having renounced all, have taken the vow of solitude, and are capable of enduring everything, are somewhat ashamed on suddenly feeling that they erroneously considered the body to be a helpmate. Those whose greatness is inconceivable, who are prepared for their work, who have adopted the seating posture (Palyankásana) for the purpose of getting rid of the (body), who have renounced delusion, meditate on a mountain, in a deep cave, or in a concealed place, (are brave) men like lions.

येषां भूषणमङ्गसंगतरजः स्थानं शिलायास्तलम्
शय्या शर्करिला मही सुविहितं गेहं गुहा द्वीपिनाम् ।
आत्मात्मीयविकल्पवीतमतयस्त्रुट्यत्तमोग्रन्थय-
स्ते नो ज्ञानधना मनांसि पुनतां मुक्तिस्पृहा निस्पृहाः ॥ २५९ ॥

259. May they purify our hearts, to whom the dust sticking to the body is an ornament, the surface of a stone a residence, gravelled earth a bed-stead, the tigers' cave a comfortable home; who have lost the erroneous notion that the soul belongs to the body; who are free from the fetters of delusion; who are possessed of the riches of knowledge; who are desireless; (and who aspire) for Liberation.

दूरारूढतपोऽनुभावजनितज्योतिः समुत्सर्पणै-
रन्तस्तत्त्वमदः कथं कथमपि प्राप्य प्रसादं गताः ।

विश्रब्धं हरिणीविलोलनयनैरापीयमाना वने
धन्यास्ते गमयन्त्यचिन्त्यचरितैर्धीराश्चिरं वासरान् ॥ २६० ॥

260. All praise be to them, who having anyhow attained (union with) the innerself, by the radiance of light produced by the influence of highly advanced austerities, have become peaceful, and are gazed at, by unsteady-eyed and confiding she-deer in the forest. Those courageous (saints) pass their days, for a long time, in inconceivable practices.

येषां बुद्धिरलक्ष्यमाणभिदयोराशात्मनोरन्तरं
गत्वोच्चैरविधाय भेदमनयोरारान्न विश्राम्यति ।
यैरन्तर्विनिवेशितः शमधनैर्बाढं बहिर्व्याप्तयः
तेषां नोऽत्र पवित्रयन्तु परमाः पादोत्थिताः पांशवः ॥ २६१ ॥

261. Whose intellect does not rest at all till it has clearly discriminated the difference, hardly perceivable, between Desire and Soul, who are rich in tranquility; and who are well fixed in the innerself and the course of whose mind does not run towards external objects—may the supremely (sacred) particles of dust, raised by the feet of such (ascetics) purify us.

यत्प्राग्जन्मनि संचितं तनुभृता कर्माशुभं वा शुभं
तद्दैवं तदुदीरणादनुभवन् दुःखं सुखं वागतम् ।
कुर्याद्यः शुभमेव सोऽप्यभिमतो यस्तूभयोच्छित्तये
सर्वारम्भपरिग्रहस्य हि परित्यागी स वन्द्यः सताम् ॥ २६२ ॥

262. Fate is the Karma, good or bad, acquired by an embodied being in past life. By their operation, the ensuing pleasure or pain is experienced. He, who performs good deeds only is praise-worthy. But he who for extirpating both (good and bad Karmas) renounces all undertakings, possessions, deserves to be adored by the good.

सुखं दुःखं वा स्यादिह विहितकर्मोदयवशात्
कुतः प्रीतिस्तापः कुत इति विकल्पाद्यदि भवेत् ।

उदासीनस्तस्य प्रगलितपुराणं न हि नवं
समास्कन्दत्येष स्फुरति सुविदग्धो मणिरिव ॥ २६३ ॥

263. In this world pleasure and pain arise out of the fruition of past Karmas. If one becomes un-attached to considerations as to whom he should have love and whom he should hate, then his past Karmas fall off, and a new on does not bind him. He, a learned (ascetic) shines forth like a jewel.

सकलविमलबोधो देहगेहे विनिर्यन्
ज्वलन इव स काष्ठं निष्ठुरं भस्मयित्वा ।
पुनरपि तदभावे प्रज्वलत्युज्ज्वलः सन्
भवति हि यतिवृत्तं सर्वथाश्चर्यभूमिः ॥ २६४ ॥

264. Like five which has completely burnt up the wood, the full pure knowledge kindled in the body-residence (of an ascetic) glows forth ablaze, even after it (the body) is gone. The life of an ascetic is all full of wonder.

गुणी गुणमयस्तस्य नाशस्तन्नाशयिष्यते ।
अतएव हि निर्वाणं शून्यमन्यैर्विकल्पितम् ॥ २६५ ॥

265. Substance is composed of attributes. The destruction of attributes, destroys substance. Hence liberation is conceived by some others as absolute non-existence (of the soul). (This is wrong).

अजातो नश्वरो मूर्त्तः कर्ता भोक्ता सुखी बुधः ।
देहमात्रो मलैर्मुक्तो गत्वोर्ध्वमचलः प्रभुः ॥ २६६ ॥

266. The soul is never born, never destroyed, (and is) immaterial. It is the doer, the enjoyer, the happy, the all-knowing and, of the size of the body, and being freed from the impurities (of Karmas), goes upwards (till the top of the universe), (and there it) remains steady and supreme.

स्वाधीन्याद्दुःखमप्यासीत्सुखं यदि तपस्विनाम् ।
स्वाधीनसुखसम्पन्ना न सिद्धाः सुखिनः कथम् ॥ २६७ ॥

**267.** If on account of independence, even pain is felt as happiness by the ascetics, then why should not the Perfect ones be happy after having acquired independent Bliss.

**इति कतिपयवाचां गोचरीकृत्य कृत्यं**
**चरितमुचितमुच्चैश्चेतसां चित्तरम्यम् ।**
**इदमविकलमन्तः सन्ततं चिन्तयन्तः**
**सपदि विपदपेतामाश्रयन्तु श्रियं ते ॥ २६८ ॥**

**268.** Charming to the hearts of the high-souled, this useful work is compiled as a collection of some words. May the adversity of those, who ponder in their hearts, continuously, over the whole of it, perish immediately and may they attain the glory (of liberation).

**जिनसेनाचार्यपादस्मरणाधीनचेतसाम् ।**
**गुणभद्रभदन्तानां कृतिरात्मानुशासनम् ॥ २६९ ॥**

**269.** Átmánushásana is the work of Guṉabhadra-Ácharya, whose heart is engaged in rememberance of the feet of his Preceptor, Jina-sena-ácharya.

**ऋषभो नाभिसूनुर्यो भूयात्स भविकाय वः ।**
**यज्ज्ञानसरसि विश्वं सरोजमिव भासते ॥ २७० ॥**

**270.** May Lord Rishabha, the son of Nabhi, in the ocean of whose knowledge the universe appears like a lotus, be for your salvation.

इति श्रीगुणभद्रभदन्तकृतमात्मानुशासनम् ।

Printed by K. D. Seth, at the Newul Kishore Press Lucknow.